The Wi-Fi Experience: Everyone's Guide to 802.11b Wireless Networking

Harold Davis

Richard Mansfield

201 W. 103rd Street
Indianapolis, Indiana 46290

CONTENTS AT A GLANCE

THE WI-FI EXPERIENCE: EVERYONE'S GUIDE TO 802.11B WIRELESS NETWORKING

International Standard Book Number: 0-7897-2662-9

Library of Congress Catalog Card Number: 2001098172

Printed in the United States of America

First Printing: December 2001

04   03   02   01   4   3   2   1

Trademarks

All terms mentioned in this book that are known to be trademarks or service marks have been appropriately capitalized. Que cannot attest to the accuracy of this information. Use of a term in this book should not be regarded as affecting the validity of any trademark or service mark.

Warning and Disclaimer

Every effort has been made to make this book as complete and as accurate as possible, but no warranty or fitness is implied. The information provided is on an "as is" basis. The author and the publisher shall have neither liability nor responsibility to any person or entity with respect to any loss or damages arising from the information contained in this book.

Associate Publisher
Dean Miller

Aquistions Editor
Angelina Ward

Development Editor
Maureen A. McDaniel

Technical Editor
Nancy Somers

Managing Editor
Thomas F. Hayes

Project Editor
Linda Seifert

Copy Editor
Sossity Smith

Proofreader
Paula Lowell

Indexer
Ken Johnson

Multimedia Developer
Michael Hunter

Team Coordinator
Sharry Lee Gregory

Production
Rebecca Harmon

Cover Designer
Bill Thomas

Interior Designer
Ruth Harvey

Contents

ABOUT THE AUTHORS

Harold Davis is currently a Managing Director at Julian Capital in Berkeley, California. He was Vice President of Strategic Development at YellowGiant Corporation, a provider of directory infrastructure software. He has served as a technology consultant to many of the most important high-technology companies, including Internet startups, Web infrastructure players, and Fortune 1000 technology companies. Harold has been a Technical Director at Vignette Corporation and a Principal in the e-commerce practice at Informix Software. In addition, he is the author of many best-selling books on programming and the Web including *Red Hat Linux 6: Visual QuickPro Guide* (Peachpit Press), *Visual Basic 6 Visual QuickStart Guide* (Peachpit Press), *Visual Basic Secrets* (IDG Books), and *Web Developer's Secrets* (IDG Books). Recently, he has written *Understanding 802.11b and Bluetooth, Enterprise Web Architecture*, and other executive briefings for MightyWords.

Richard Mansfield (High Point, NC) is an author and programmer whose recent titles include *Visual Basic .NET ASP.NET Programming* (Hungry Minds) and *Visual Basic .NET Database Programming For Dummies* (Hungry Minds). While he was the editor of *COMPUTE! Magazine* during the '80s, he wrote hundreds of magazine articles and two monthly columns. From 1987 to 1991, Richard was editorial director and partner in Signal Research. He began writing books full-time in 1991, and has written 28 computer books. Over 500,000 of his books have been sold worldwide and have been translated into 11 languages.

DEDICATION

To Jim Coward, David Lee Roach, and Larry O'Connor.

> *—Richard Mansfield*

To my children: Julian and Nicholas.

> *—Harold Davis*

ACKNOWLEDGMENTS

First, we'd like to thank Acquisitions Editor Angelina Ward for her thoughtful advice. Development Editor Maureen McDaniel deserves credit for her discernment, and the high quality of her editing. Technical Editor Nancy Somers carefully reviewed the entire manuscript and made important suggestions. Project Editor Linda Seifert ensured that this book moved smoothly through production, and Sossity Smith, Copy Editor, combed through every line of our text and made a number of improvements. To all these, and the other good people at Que who contributed to this book, our thanks for the enhancements they made to this book.

A book covering cutting-edge technology benefits significantly from expert opinions and predictions. We were fortunate to have interviewed some of the best brains in the field of wireless networking. We thank the following experts for contributing their expertise: Jim LeValley of CISCO, Brian Grimm of WECA, Mark Shapiro at Lucent, Jay Dominick of Wake Forest University, Ali Tabasi of MobileStar, Chris Stacey of The Venetian Hotel, John Wise of Springbok Cohn & Wolfe, and Brewster Kahle of Alexa and SFLAN.

In addition, the authors would like to give special thanks to their agent, Matt Wagner, of Waterside Productions, whose contributions to this book were above and beyond the call of duty.

TELL US WHAT YOU THINK!

As the reader of this book, *you* are our most important critic and commentator. We value your opinion and want to know what we're doing right, what we could do better, what areas you'd like to see us publish in, and any other words of wisdom you're willing to pass our way.

As an Associate Publisher for Que, I welcome your comments. You can fax, e-mail, or write me directly to let me know what you did or didn't like about this book—as well as what we can do to make our books stronger.

Please note that I cannot help you with technical problems related to the topic of this book, and that due to the high volume of mail I receive, I might not be able to reply to every message.

When you write, please be sure to include this book's title and author as well as your name and phone or fax number. I will carefully review your comments and share them with the author and editors who worked on the book.

Fax: 317-581-4666
E-mail: feedback@quepublishing.com
Mail: Dean Miller
          Que
          201 West 103rd Street
          Indianapolis, IN 46290 USA

INTRODUCTION

Amid the general tech collapse, there's one rising star: Wi-Fi, wireless networking. Its sales are going through the roof and its costs have plummeted. Why? Because where computers are useful, networks are often useful, too.

The only problem with traditional networks is their wires: You have to run lots of ethernet wires in brand-new buildings (expensive), or retrofit existing buildings (*very* expensive). The solution is wireless networking and Wi-Fi—802.11b, to use its official name—is far and away the most popular wireless solution today.

Here are some of the main benefits of Wi-Fi:

- **Inexpensive**—You can create a wireless network between your home computers for less than $200.
- **Useful**—You can remain connected to the Internet, other computers, and printers anywhere within the Wi-Fi broadcasting area.
- **Scalable**—Wi-Fi can service anything from two home computers to the whole Stanford University campus. Wi-Fi can either extend an existing wire network, or build a new network from scratch.
- **Wise**—Those in the know are using Wi-Fi, shouldn't you? Microsoft uses Wi-Fi to connect its entire Seattle campus.

This book shows you the ins and outs of Wi-Fi. You'll learn how to install everything from a small home network to a large office system. And we don't simply give you general, abstract advice. You'll find step-by-step instructions that will take you by the hand from start to successful finish.

You'll find case studies throughout the book, illustrating the many ways that people are using Wi-Fi networking. You'll also see how to connect your network to the Internet (cable modem, broadband DSL, ordinary modem, what have you). Chapter 2, "Setting Up Your Personal Wireless Network," and Chapter 3, "Larger Scale Wi-Fi Setups," show you how to survey your needs, decide which equipment to purchase, and complete the installation. In Chapter 6, "Putting an Antenna on Your Roof and Elsewhere," you'll see how to tell whether your network would benefit from antennas, and, if so, how to install them. If you're concerned about security, Chapter 8, "Security and Encryption," explores this topic in depth—covering everything from Wireless Equivalent Privacy to firewalls. We tell you what works and what doesn't. Finally, Chapter 9, "The Wi-Fi Revolution," looks to the future of Wi-Fi: improved security, higher speeds, backward compatibility with today's equipment, and other issues.

We've tried to accomplish the following three main goals in this book:

- To make setting up your Wi-Fi network—large or small—an easy, painless, and quick process. We've been there, done that, and learned some painful lessons along the way. We spent *an entire day* setting up a single access point to broadcast a cable modem Internet connection throughout a house. Because we spent that day, you should be able to avoid the problems we encountered—and get yours up and running in less than an hour (see Chapter 5, "The Internet Connection"). Likewise, we spent almost a whole day installing a Wi-Fi peer-to-peer LAN (local area network). It shouldn't take you anywhere near that much time if you follow the steps described in Chapter 2.

- To cut through the marketing hype. For example, if you will have problems setting up a Wi-Fi LAN in a library—and you will—we tell you the facts. We also tell you the solution (you'll need extra access points, and perhaps outboard antennas placed high on the walls). We tell you how to conduct a site survey to make it easier to install Wi-Fi in large offices. We provide case studies throughout the book illustrating various ways people are successfully using Wi-Fi: how hotels, coffee shops, homes, schools, legal offices, airports, and others are benefiting from their Wi-Fi installations.

- To explain the technology without throwing useless factoids at you, or lecturing you with boring data you don't need to know. We cut to the chase. You probably *do* need to understand the weaknesses of current Wi-Fi security measures, for instance. And you need answers: how to protect sensitive data from listeners who are more than happy to sit on a bench outside your offices and tune into your Wi-Fi radio broadcasts. We believe that you'll find our discussion of authentication, firewalls, encryption, and other Wi-Fi security-related topics interesting and valuable. Read Chapter 8 to see if you think we've succeeded.

We've found ourselves caught up in the excitement and power of the Wi-Fi revolution. It's one of the very few bright lights in the general technology downturn. Prices for Wi-Fi gear have come way down as sales have taken off. It costs very little now to join this revolution, and we hope that this book will convince you of the many benefits of what techies call 802.11b, but what most of us call *Wi-Fi*.

If you want to join the Wi-Fi revolution, this book will explain it all to you in plain English.

CHAPTER

1

UNDERSTANDING WI-FI

In this chapter

Wireless networking, dominated by Wi-Fi, is rapidly replacing or extending traditional wire networks in homes, campuses, and offices everywhere.

Wi-Fi is now more cost effective than wired networks in most situations, and Wi-Fi offers more benefits to users. For example, users gain the freedom to roam with their computers, yet remain connected to their local network or to the Internet. You can also save considerable money every month by sharing a single Wi-Fi Internet connection among multiple users.

Wi-Fi is an excellent, inexpensive way to quickly network your desktop to your portable at home—plus you gain the freedom to take your portable all around the house and even outside on the deck, patio, or, if you're really wealthy, your *esplanade*.

And Wi-Fi is quite scalable: It works as well for a university such as Wake Forest, where it serves thousands, as it does for two or three machines in your home. Don't assume that you have too few computers to make Wi-Fi useful. It's very inexpensive, and you'll quickly find value in this technology when your portable can easily use the printer attached to your desktop, among many other synergies.

However, as with many technologies, the marketing of Wi-Fi sometimes involves a bit of snake oil salesmanship. Step right up! You've probably seen those dubious (to use the polite word) pages-per-minute claims made by printer manufacturers. Well, in the world of Wi-Fi marketing, it's the transmission rates and range of communication specs that are regularly, shamelessly exaggerated.

The official transmission rate, for example, quoted by most Wi-Fi manufacturers is 11Mbps (megabits per second). Yeah, and I can do a one minute mile with a rocket pack. Down here in the real world, transmission rates average closer to 4Mbps, sometimes less.

You'll also hear claims that you can just *plug and play* your Wi-Fi units. True, Wi-Fi is generally quite a bit easier to install than a traditional wire network. But the confusing or incomplete documentation that comes with most Wi-Fi equipment is not, sadly, up to the standards of the hardware that it attempts, and usually fails, to describe.

In this book we'll tell you the truth about both the limitations and the capabilities of Wi-Fi. You'll find both general concepts and specific recommendations. We cover everything from the standards, history, and politics of Wi-Fi to how you can make the smartest purchasing decisions. Above all, we've worked hard to ensure that the information in this book is objective.

WHAT IS WIRELESS NETWORKING?

Perhaps you don't care that much about standards, or the politics of standards. That's fine. If your main interest is in the practical nuts and bolts of setting up your own home or office wireless network, feel free to skip right to Chapter 2, "Setting Up Your Personal Wireless Network." On the other hand, if you'd like to learn the basics, and a little history, about this quiet revolution in networking, you'll find it in this chapter.

"Wi-Fi"—or "wireless fidelity," the informal name given to the IEEE 802.11b High Rate standard—has the potential for consumer popularity comparable to the early days of the PC.

Wireless networking is, as you probably know or can easily figure out, networking without wires. It's been around a while using older, somewhat proprietary standards, but with 802.11b, or Wi-Fi, it has really come of age.

Wireless networks have many advantages over wire line networks. They are cheaper to set up because you don't have to knock down walls (or run wires). Where you work is more flexible because you don't need a network plug to be handy. With the widespread proliferation of Wi-Fi, it makes a great deal of sense for both businesses and homes to set up wireless networks.

CH

1

Note

Wi-Fi *per se* is just a specification for wireless networking promulgated by the IEEE Standards Association, `http://standards.ieee.org/`. The IEEE likes to designate standards using numbers, rather than names. Within the IEEE schema, the number 802 is used to designate local area networks and metropolitan area networks (LANs and WANs). 802.11 is the name for wireless LAN specifications in general, and 802.11b is a particular version of the wireless LAN specification that runs on the 2.4GHz (gigahertz) spectrum at high speeds (up to 11Mbps). The Federal Communications Commission has reserved the 2.4GHz spectrum primarily for home appliances such as microwaves and cordless phones.

Wi-Fi is a wireless implementation of packet-based (IP) networking at speeds that are comparable to 10BASE-T. In other words, the Wi-Fi part of your connection is not going to slow down your Web surfing.

Many times, Wi-Fi is cheaper and has more functional advantages than wired networking.

What applications are going to be written on top of Wi-Fi? Things get interesting when applications such as Voice over IP (VoIP) get layered on top of 802.11b. Could a pieced-together grassroots network based on 802.11b and VoIP replace the commercial voice cell phone net? Stranger things have happened. Wi-Fi has stimulated the idealistic free Internet access rhetoric that has not been heard since the early days of the wired Internet.

THE 2.4 GIGAHERTZ SPECTRUM

Wi-Fi (802.11b) runs on the 2.4GHz spectrum, which is unlicensed by the Federal Communications Commission (FCC) . Spectrums that are unlicensed are also called "free," because anyone can use them.

2.4GHz was originally intended for appliances such as microwave ovens and cordless phones. Besides Wi-Fi, one other important wireless standard, Bluetooth, has been designed to run on this spectrum.

This means that one potential issue is *spectrum conflict*. Will Wi-Fi, Bluetooth, and other appliances designed to run on 2.4GHz interfere with one another's ability to communicate? So far, there don't seem to be any huge problems with this, but some professional network administrators have banned Bluetooth (and cordless phones) from environments that count on Wi-Fi.

BLUETOOTH

In contrast to Wi-Fi, which easily extends hundreds of feet (more with specialized equipment), Bluetooth is intended for appliance-to-appliance communication of not more than thirty feet. (Think of it as the infrared beaming mechanism intended for data exchange between PDAs on steroids.) Bluetooth is also far slower than Wi-Fi.

Bluetooth is best thought of as a personal-area network intended to allow devices to inter-operate (as compared to Wi-Fi, which is intended for wireless *local* area networks). The idea behind Bluetooth is to allow devices to interoperate seamlessly. A classic hypothetical example would be a Bluetooth-enabled PDA that automatically synchs with your desktop PC. Other uses might include Bluetooth-enabled wireless peripherals, cell phone earpieces, and so on. So the conception behind Bluetooth is "cutting wires"—not creating wireless networks.

Bluetooth began as a 1994 initiative by Swedish telecom (telecommunications) giant Ericsson. Ericsson was interested in exploring inexpensive radio interfaces between cell phones and their accessories.

A few years later, Ericsson, together with IBM, Intel, Nokia, and Toshiba, founded the Bluetooth Special Interest Group (SIG) , www.bluetooth.com/.

The name "Bluetooth" comes from a historical figure, the fierce tenth-century Danish warrior King Harald. Harald's nickname was Bluetooth, the term for a discolored tooth that has been deprived of blood (dentistry not being all that it could be in the tenth century).

The current version of the Bluetooth specification is divided into two parts, Core and Profile.

The *Core* part, over 1,000 pages, specifies components such as the radio, baseband, link manager, service discovery protocol, transport layer, and interoperability with different communication protocols.

The *Profile* part, close to 500 pages, specifies the protocols and procedures required for different types of Bluetooth applications. It is organized by application type presented essentially as case studies: cordless telephony, fax intercom, headset, and so on. For example, the Fax Profile "...defines the protocols and procedures that shall be used by the fax part of the usage model...."

Any Bluetooth system has four necessary parts: a radio that receives and transmits data and voice, a baseband or link control unit that processes the transmitted or received data, link management software that manages the transmission, and supporting application software.

As of today, there are several thousand corporate members of the Bluetooth SIG. But few, if any, Bluetooth products have actually shipped. Apart from concerns about interference in the 2.4GHz spectrum, and negative comparisons with 802.11b's range and speed, the primary issue seems to be cost.

Bluetooth was initially promoted on the basis of ubiquity and low cost. Currently, Bluetooth radios cost about $40 each. To be commercially feasible, industry experts have suggested that the price must fall to about $5 per unit. As industry volume ramps, and Moore's law comes into play, it's certain that unit prices will fall, but, of course, the question is when. Industry experts suggest that the $5 unit cost per radio will be achieved sometime between 2003 and 2005.

In the meantime, while Bluetooth stagnates, well, like a tooth cut off from blood, Wi-Fi proliferates. Proliferation means that Wi-Fi devices get cheaper and cheaper. Although the two technologies can complement each other and work well together, if Wi-Fi devices are actually as cheap as Bluetooth, it's hard to see much rationale for Bluetooth, which is far slower, and has far less range. Bluetooth's effective indoor range is only 10 or 11 yards, compared to Wi-Fi's typical 50- to 100-yard range.

802.11B

802.11b is the engineering, nontrademarked name for Wi-Fi. WECA, the trade association that "owns" the Wi-Fi name, certifies standards compliance as explained later in this chapter in the section "WECA and Wi-Fi" (so, by all means, buy Wi-Fi certified 802.11b gear).

802.11b is an intermediate-range wireless networking standard that runs at speeds comparable to standard ethernet. The 802.11b specification includes a Medium Access Control layer and a Physical layer using Direct Sequence Spread Spectrum technology.

The most immediate, obvious, and important application for 802.11b is wireless networking. If you've ever had to drill through walls to install a network, you'll appreciate that it's a lot easier and less expensive to use 802.11b wireless connectivity than to run wires, knock down walls, and do all that messy stuff. Because 802.11b runs at speeds comparable to 10BASE-T ethernet, there's really no performance trade-off for this convenience. In addition, 802.11b connects to laptops that are in the yard, on the roof, or beside the pool, not just fixed cubicle workstations. Finally, 802.11b is an ideal technology for implementing networking in places such as coffee shops and hotel lobbies.

802.11b networks have been installed in major corporate campuses, offices of all sizes, universities and schools, and in homes. In many cases, there's a kind of viral adoption in which 802.11b networks are grafted onto existing corporate LANs on an ad hoc basis.

To set up an 802.11b, you need an Access Point (AP) such as Apple's AirPort or Cisco's Aironet. The Access Point can connect to existing LAN resources, such as a switch or router. It then serves as a wireless router, potentially allowing access to any computer equipped with an 802.11b card that is within range.

Because even under ideal conditions the 802.11b range is limited to 300 feet, most extensive 802.11b networks require multiple Access Points, which can be spaced out so that all likely areas have coverage. Rooftop antennas and amplifying technology can also increase range.

It has been said that 802.11b has set the cause of network security back at least 10 years. To understand why, consider that any mobile computer equipped with an 802.11b PCMIA card can potentially connect through an Access Point to internal network resources. This means you could connect to an unprotected corporate network from the street in front of the building.

Proper security precautions include using wireless encryption (WEP), even though this slows 802.11b transmission rates and WEP security, alas, is not difficult to break. In addition, internal network resources should be protected from Access Points with a firewall. Users should only be able to obtain access through the firewall following authentication. We'll get into detail in Chapter 8, "Security and Encryption," about the steps you can take to improve Wi-Fi LAN security.

One of the most enticing aspects of 802.11b is its enabling of anytime, anywhere networking. (Whether you really want to work while you're poolside is another question.) In this spirit, Starbucks has announced that it will deploy 802.11b in about 70% of its 4,000 North American locations. Anyone with an 802.11b card in his or her laptop will be able to go into Starbucks for a latte and surf the Web (see the discussion of Wi-Fi at Starbucks in Chapter 7, "Lighting Up the Neighborhood").

Another example of a mobile application using 802.11b is a guest check-in application being launched by the Venetian Hotel in Las Vegas.

Hotel clerks will meet guests at building entrances, confirm their reservations via an 802.11b connection to a network server, and hand them keys on the spot. The goal is to eliminate check-in lines.

This particular application will use handheld devices that run the Palm OS and are strapped to the hotel clerks' wrists. The handheld device includes a magnetic reader for credit cards, and the clerks will also carry an encoder for the room-key cards. Because of the huge room turnover at the Venetian, real-time connectivity to the central server is required to be sure that room assignments are current.

For more information on the Venetian Hotel application, see Chapter 4, "At Home and At Work."

THE POLITICS AND ECONOMICS OF 802.11B

Some of the same free spirits who spurred the explosive growth of the Internet and participated in the Open Source programming movement have found 802.11b. "Because 802.11b is a license-free technology," the thinking goes, "why not set up cooperative metropolitan area networks that are not beholden to the global telecommunications players?"

The free 802.11b movement is international, but it is particularly active on the "left" (or West) coast of the United States, where wireless users' group meetings are standing-room-only affairs. For a list of 802.11b community networks, see `www.toaster.net/wireless/community.html`.

One of the most influential 802.11b community networks is SFLAN, the brainchild of Internet entrepreneur Brewster Kahle. As a test case, SFLAN has successfully 802.11b-enabled San Francisco's Presidio neighborhood using coffee shops, a bowling alley, and a daycare center as Access Points. SFLAN is described in detail in Chapter 7 of this book.

THE ROLE OF THE IEEE

The IEEE (Institute of Electrical and Electronic Engineers) Standards Association, `http://standards.ieee.org/`, is a nonprofit organization intended to help "advance global prosperity by promoting the engineering process of creating, developing, integrating, sharing, and applying knowledge about electrical and information technologies and sciences for the benefit of humanity and the profession."

One of the IEEE's primary activities is to help develop and promulgate technology standards. The organization likes to designate standards using numbers rather than names. Within the IEEE schema, the number 802 is used to designate local area networks and metropolitan, or wide, area networks (LANs and WANs). 802.11 is the name for wireless LAN specifications in general, and 802.11b is the particular version of the wireless LAN specification that runs on the 2.4GHz spectrum at high speeds.

Going back to 802.11, it's important to understand the purpose of the general wireless LAN standardAccording to the original Project Authorization" Request, "the scope of the proposed standard is to develop a specification for wireless connectivity for fixed, portable, and moving stations within a local area." In addition, "…the purpose of the standard is to provide wireless connectivity to automatic machinery and equipment or stations that require rapid deployment, which may be portable, handheld, or which may be mounted on moving vehicles within a local area."

The standard specifies two important parts, or layers: the Medium Access Control (MAC) and Physical (PHY). The MAC layer is a set of protocols that are responsible for maintaining order in the use of a shared medium. For example, data encryption is handled in the MAC.

The PHY layerhandles transmission between nodes. In other words, it is primarily concerned with hardware.

These layers fit within the generalized OSI—Open System Interconnection—reference model. The OSI model is a way of describing how different applications and protocols interact on network-aware devices.

The primary purpose of 802.11 is to deliver MAC Service Data Units (MSDUs) between Logical Link Controls (LLCs). Essentially, an LLC is a base station with a wireless access point, which itself may be connected to a wire line network for hand-off to additional wireless LLCs.

802.11 networks operate in one of two modes:

Infrastructure—The infrastructure is architecture is used to provide network communications between wireless clients and wired network resources.

Ad Hoc—An ad hoc network architecture is used to support mutual communication between wireless clients. It is typically created spontaneously, does not support access to wired networks, and does not require an access point to be part of the network.

The PHY layer of 802.11 defines three physical characteristics for wireless local area networks:

- Diffused Infrared
- Direct Sequence Spread Spectrum (DSSS)
- Frequency Hopping Spread Spectrum (FHSS)

DSSS and FHSS are fundamentally incompatible. 802.11b is an extension of 802.11 that standardizes on DSSS rather than FHSS. This has boosted network throughput speeds to a theoretical 11 Mbps (by comparison, slightly faster than the 10-Mbps throughput of a wired 10BaseT Ethernet network). For this reason, 802.11b is sometimes also called *802.11 DSSS* or *802.11 High Rate* or "802.11 High Rate.

By the way, the 11Mbps throughput is a theoretical maximum and is rarely maintained for a number of reasons. Transmission rates go down as signals get weaker, or as interference increases. Encryption slows things down. Access point connections are a bottleneck (and typically only connect you to a 10Mbps network anyway). Most 802.11b client cards on the market only support half-duplex communication (they have one radio in them), meaning that your device can talk, or listen, but not both at the same time.

The 802.11 standard and the 802.11b standard extensions are a moving target. They evolve as time goes by. The current version can be viewed by subscription and/or by IEEE members (see http://standards.ieee.org/ for details). However, a new IEEE program makes a slightly dated version of the standards available to the public for free. These documents are available in Adobe Acrobat format at http://standards.ieee.org/getieee802/802.11.html.

To be noted: Not only is the target moving, it is also big. The underlying 802.11 specification document is more than 500 pages long, and the 802.11b extension specifications are substantial as well.

WECA AND WI-FI

Wi-Fi—short for *wireless fidelity*—is the name given to a specific flavor of 802.11b by a trade organization, the Wireless Ethernet Compatibility Alliance (WECA), www.wirelessethernet.org/index.html.

WECA's mission is to "certify interoperability of Wi-Fi... products and to promote Wi-Fi as the global wireless LAN standard across all market segments." To join, a company needs to have a "legitimate business interest," to support the IEEE 802.11b standard, and to pay annual dues of $20,000. In other words, pretty much anyone who has any significant interest in wireless networking can join. Members include companies such as Apple, Cisco, and Intersil.

It's worth noting that the term *Wi-Fi* is owned (and trademarked) by WECA. Essentially, WECA's reason for being is to promote Wi-Fi through educational and lobbying activities as well as through interoperability certification. It's the goal of WECA to have consumers identify the Wi-Fi logo as a wireless interoperability "Good Housekeeping" seal of approval.

Nobody other than a hard-core engineer type could be terribly fond of the term *802.11b* to designate a technology and movement. So *Wi-Fi* seems a bit more user-friendly term to use.

You can find the complete list of Wi-Fi certified 802.11b products at `www.wirelessethernet.org/certified_products.asp`.

802.11B AND 3G

3G—third generation—wireless is a proposed high-speed broadband network for data transmission to cellular devices. 3G actually refers to speed (and, perhaps, a vision of the future) rather than specifications and spectrums. There are plans to implement 3G using two flavors of Code Division Multiple Access (CDMA): CDMA2000 and Wideband CDMA (W-CDMA) cellular networks.

3G is expected to provide wireless services at up to 384 Mbps—more than 30 times faster than 802.11b, and hundreds of times faster than Internet access on today's cell phones. In addition, the range of this signal will be comparable to today's cell phone networks; in other words, substantially greater than anything 802.11 offers. 3G will run over existing telecom-purchased spectrum and spectrum purchased (at great expense) solely for this purpose.

If Bluetooth is intended for personal, short-range networking, and 802.11b is best for medium-range local area networking, then 3G is the science fiction solution: long distance, and with a fat pipe.

3G is more a vision, and a migration, than a unified standard or spectrum. The truth of the matter is that each major telecom wireless infrastructure will wend its own way toward 3G. The networks will come from different starting places, will have different stops along the way (dubbed 2.5G), and may not have the same end point.

3G is a catchall term for a pie-in-the-sky technology that, according to the *Wall Street Journal*, has already cost European telecoms over $100 billion for spectrum alone. It's estimated that the monthly per-user incremental cost to cover spectrum licenses and infrastructure would have to be at least $100. Telecoms must figure out what applications they can build to entice users and justify the expense and the monthly cost to users. Would you pay $100 a month extra for fancy wireless applications on your cell phone? We didn't think so. It's the exact opposite of the Wi-Fi situation, which is "good enough, cheap, and ready now."

CHAPTER 2

SETTING UP YOUR PERSONAL WIRELESS NETWORK

In this chapter

This chapter explains how to set up the simplest, least expensive wireless network using 802.11b (Wi-Fi) technology. By *simplest*, we mean the fewest physical units: merely client cards; no access points or external antennas. Also, you can get a Wi-Fi local area network (LAN) up and running for about $200–300, street price.

Even though this chapter covers how to set up a small Wi-Fi installation in a home or small office, a few of the topics we'll cover here are, paradoxically, the most complicated in this entire book.

Caution

> Before going any further, I want to give you the best advice I've discovered concerning installing Wi-Fi equipment: Go to the manufacturer's Web site and download *all* the *latest* software for your Wi-Fi unit. In many hours of testing with various manufacturers' Wi-Fi equipment, I've found one nearly universal rule: Your installation will go much more smoothly if you download the support software from the manufacturer's Web site rather than relying on the software on the CD that ships with the equipment.
>
> There are several reasons for this. Wi-Fi is a relatively new technology and drivers are being frequently revised to remove bugs. Most Wi-Fi equipment requires at least three items of software: A driver, utility (setup and management) software, and a firmware update file. *Often, each of these programs must be the same version.* In other words, you cannot use a new driver with older firmware.

Most large offices already have a wire network installed. In a large office, all you have to do is *add* the Wi-Fi units to the existing network. Small offices not only need the Wi-Fi, they also need the underlying network as well.

In a large office you add transceivers (the "access point" peripherals) to put the existing wire network on the air. Adding access points to an existing network is the topic of Chapter 3.

Here, in Chapter 2, we're going to explain both how to add the Wi-Fi client peripherals, and also how to create and manage a Windows Peer-to-Peer network.

This chapter covers what is potentially the most complex job for someone installing a Wi-Fi LAN. Why? Because in addition to dealing with the Wi-Fi technology itself, you also have to set up a network using various Windows networking technologies.

HOW MUCH DOES IT COST?

Quality Wi-Fi PCM cards can be bought for as little as $99, and the prices are dropping as Wi-Fi increases in popularity. These flat, little cards are somewhat thicker, and about 30% longer, than a credit card. They slide into external slots found on most portable computers sold in the past several years. For your desktop computer, you can buy an adapter for about $40. It's a PCI card that you insert inside your computer's case. It's an adapter; its sole function is to accept a Wi-Fi PCM card.

CH
2

The most basic Wi-Fi setup, then, involves putting an adapter into your desktop machine, sticking a PCM card into that adapter, and sticking a second PCM card into your laptop (which needs no adapter because it already has a PCM port built in).

Actually, to be honest, there is an even *simpler* Wi-Fi setup involving the new USB Wi-Fi devices (see the following Tip).

Then, after you deal with the software issues (*not* a trivial task in most cases, unfortunately) your desktop machine and the laptop connected in this simple Wi-Fi LAN arrangement can see each other's directories; share files, printers, and other peripherals; even run some of each other's programs and otherwise communicate, just as if they were wired together, or were one big machine. You can also play games over your Wi-Fi LAN. The connected computers employ the Microsoft Networking Files and Printer Sharing features, as you'll see later in this chapter. In summary: Wi-Fi units are capable of performing all the same tasks as ordinary, old-fashioned wired LANs.

Tip

If you want to save some money, really hate the idea of opening up your desktop machine to insert the adapter card + PCM card, and would like the flexibility offered by an outboard Wi-Fi unit, read on. For about $120, you can avoid the adapter card + PCM card approach. Take a different route: Buy an outboard USB unit that simply plugs into one of your desktop's USB ports. Manufacturers are just now starting to offer USB Wi-Fi units. Two of the best are LinkSys's model WUSB11, and the ORiNOCO USB Client. (Note that most recent desktop computers come with two USB ports, but if you've already used up those ports already with existing peripherals, you can get a 4-port USB adapter for around $20.)

So, the simplest physical Wi-Fi setup is two computers, each with a wireless "network adapter" (client unit) plugged into one of its ports. Notice that this approach does not require a Wi-Fi *Access Point* unit or any other additional hardware.

(Access points and other heavy-duty Wi-Fi hardware are the topics of the next chapter. Chapter 3, "Larger Scale Wi-Fi Setups," is for people interested in "lighting up" a large office, a whole neighborhood, or, as some people in San Francisco are trying to do: lighting up a *whole city*).

Simple Wi-Fi setups can be extremely simple, and flexible as well. For example, if you want to play a computer game against a friend, you can take your notebook computers out by the pool and not worry about having to *wire* them together physically somehow (very old-fashioned).

Instead, just slip two PCM cards into the two notebooks and you're ready to play.

After you've installed the Wi-Fi PCM card support software from the manufacturer and created the workgroup (that is, established a Windows Peer-to-Peer network to which the two notebooks belong), you can then freely mix and match all your home or small office computers. If you don't have PCM cards (or USB units) for each computer, simply unplug a

PCM card from a machine you aren't using and plug the card into a machine you want to "go Wi-Fi." With the software already configured, making a machine communicate via Wi-Fi is a simple as inserting the PCM card, or plugging in the USB unit (USB units can be used with either desktop machines or laptops).

With Wi-Fi, you can cross platforms, too. Windows 2000 machines can seamlessly work with Windows 98 or Me machines, for example. In this chapter we'll describe how to set up a Wi-Fi LAN, and underlying networks, in both Windows 2000 and Windows 98/Me.

All Wi-Fi adapters—PCM or USB—have a built in *transceiver* (a combination *transmission* antenna to send messages out, and *receiving* antenna to accept messages being broadcast by other machines—usually the same physical antenna). If you want your desktop and portable to be able to talk to each other (or several desktops, several portables or any combination thereof), you can easily and cheaply get them communicating via Wi-Fi (see Figure 2.1).

Figure 2.1
The simplest Wi-Fi setup involves two computers, each with a PCM transceiver unit attached. These two notebooks are communicating wirelessly, using PCM cards.

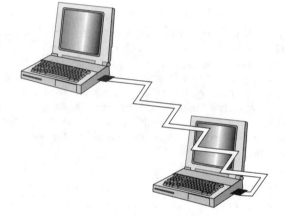

BENEFITS OF A HOME OR SMALL OFFICE WI-FI NETWORK

Before getting down to the steps you should take to install a small Wi-Fi system, let's consider the reasons you might want to join your computers into a network, particularly a wireless network.

This chapter focuses on the home and small office user, sometimes called *SOHO* (Small Office Home Office). There are several reasons to network a SOHO. Various efficiencies result when you can share resources such as an Internet connection or a printer between several computers. Also, it's easier to share files between machines in a local area network (you don't have to transfer them to a diskette or some other physical medium). However, file sharing is less of a problem these days than it used to be, before the Internet. It's now pretty easy now to share files by simply attaching them to e-mail messages (even if you're only communicating to someone just across the room).

Speaking of Internet access, a Wi-Fi home network can support multiple, *simultaneous* high-speed Internet connections from your several SOHO computers (these connections can be cable modem or DSL). You will see how to add Internet connections to your Wi-Fi network in Chapter 5, "The Internet Connection." *What* a modern house you have! Dad can be in the kitchen downloading a Martha Stewart Good Thing Pie recipe while Mom and the kids are playing Quake against each other from their respective bedrooms!

Traditional wired networks have several disadvantages. First, you obviously have to string wires. Even though wired networking hardware units are at first less expensive than the equivalent Wi-Fi units, in the long run, when the actual wiring costs are factored in, Wi-Fi can be significantly less expensive. And a wired network is far more difficult to modify later on.

Historic buildings with treasured murals, schools with asbestos insulation or other "do not disturb" environmental problems find wiring a particular difficulty (see Chapter 7, "Lighting Up the Neighborhood").

Also, Wi-Fi is highly adaptable—you can put computers where you want them, easily rearrange them, and wander, moving around freely within the Wi-Fi coverage zone with a laptop. Wi-Fi-connected computers are highly portable. And people using a Wi-Fi laptop in an organization become more *mobile*. How much this freedom contributes to increased productivity remains to be tested, but that it does contribute is not in doubt.

Needless to say, a Wi-Fi-enabled machine can be used in many places that a wired machine cannot: patio, unwired conference room, rooftop, whatever. Connections are always on.

Finally, Wi-Fi is far more *scalable* than the alternative LAN installations. You can reconfigure to meet new needs. You can quickly ramp up (scale up) from a simple Peer-to-Peer setup (an average network load limits this approach to 10 machines maximum) to a full "infrastructure" network with thousands of users, covering a wide "roaming" area.

The next chapter ramps things up. For now, let's get a modest little SOHO Wi-Fi zone lit up and working. Technically, the active coverage area (the area within which communication is possible) in a wireless LAN is called a *microcell*. This is similar to the cell phone system that also involves such concepts as overlapping "cell" areas, "roaming" from cell to cell, and so on. Wi-Fi LAN and cell phones operate in somewhat similar ways to extend the area of continuous coverage beyond the zone of a single cell.

UNDERSTANDING RANGE

How large an area is covered by the simplest Wi-Fi LAN Peer-to-Peer setup (one using PCM cards, but no additional hardware—no access point units, or antennas)?

A good quality Wi-Fi PCM card can reach a maximum access of around 500 feet, if conditions are perfect. This figure is only true in a mostly *unobstructed* environment—such as a newsroom with desks, but no cubicles. If you put your face down next to one of the inserted PCM cards on one computer, you should be able to physically *see* the card in the other networked computer. That's what line-of-sight means. In other words, the 500-foot range is line-of-sight with no interference from competition in the Wi-Fi band (microwave ovens, 2.4GHz wireless phones, nearby radio stations).

AUTOMATIC SLOWDOWN

To deal with the weaker signals involved when there is significant distance between two Wi-Fi units, most Wi-Fi equipment employs what is known as *automatic scale back* technology. The speed of a Wi-Fi connection is automatically slowed down as its signal gets weaker—as the distance between communicating computers grows larger. You can see this happening if you walk your portable away from another computer it's communicating with over a Wi-Fi LAN. (A weaker signal has more noise and the communication must be slowed down to ensure accuracy.) To see the effect, run the utility software that came with your Wi-Fi unit as you walk your portable computer around to different locations.

MEASURING DATA RATES: HOW FAST IS FAST ENOUGH?

Several factors can degrade Wi-Fi communication speeds (or *throughput*). Note that throughput means the amount of data that can be transmitted in a given time. Various factors influence throughput including interference and the number of people actively using the Wi-Fi network. To understand throughput, we should first consider the relationship between speed of Wi-Fi transmission and the distance between antennas.

INDOOR COVERAGE

Here's how automatic scale back retards signal transfer rate to compensate for a weakened (long distance) indoor signal, when using good quality Wi-Fi hardware. Note that Wi-Fi transmission and data throughput figures are always *best case*, so in real installations you can expect to achieve lesser results:

Speed	Distance
11Mbps	Up to 160 ft.
5.5Mbps	Up to 260 ft.
2Mbps	Up to 390 ft.
1Mbps	Up to 490 ft.

OUTDOOR COVERAGE

The outdoor environment is inherently superior for the transmission of signals—fewer devices competing for the same bandwidth, fewer obstructions, and so on. All things being equal, you'll get better radio reception, for example, if you put an antenna outside on your roof, rather than inside your attic. The greater "purity" of outside communications results in more generous outdoor coverage.

Here's how automatic scale back retards signal transfer rate outdoors:

Speed	Distance
11Mbps	Up to 820 ft.
5.5Mbps	Up to 1,150 ft.
2Mbps	Up to 1,300 ft.
1Mbps	Up to 1,640 ft.

Don't be discouraged, though, even if you find yourself reduced to 1Mbps—that's still a fast transfer rate. You may well notice significant slowdown when accessing a remote computer's drive or directory listings, when transferring very large files or while accessing a high-speed Internet connection.

But perceived speed is often relative. Most people are currently surfing the Internet at 56 Kbps (this is approximately 56,000 bits per second versus the Wi-Fi rate of 1,024,000 bits per second). Even high-speed Internet connections (T1, ASDL, cable modem) top out at 1.5Mbps, again, under ideal conditions. So Wi-Fi's "worst case" 1Mbps scale back isn't really that slow at all, comparatively.

The widely reported 11Mbps data rate is actually theoretical. Actual throughput is closer to 4Mbps. And if you have quite a few people using the connection, 4 might simply not be enough. We'll have more to say about what to do to solve sluggish Wi-Fi communications in the next chapter, but note that there *are* solutions. You can add access points (up to three can be used in the same coverage area), which effectively boosts the nominal rate to 33Mbps. When you do something like this, you subdivide the users into three different workgroups using three different channels. There are other tactics as well, not to mention that fairly soon (some claim as soon as late 2001), the new standard, 802.11a, will emerge, operating at 54Mbps. In addition to being five times faster than today's 802.11b Wi-Fi standard, 11a doesn't suffer from the interference that can plague some 11b installations (11a operates in a different band: 5.8GHz). We'll have more to say about the 11a technology in Chapter 9, "The Wi-Fi Revolution."

Don't bother your head with these issues now. This chapter is all about a SOHO setup, and you're likely to be quite satisfied with the typical available throughput in a home or small office.

SEEING SPEED

Most Wi-Fi hardware comes with utility software you can use to see the current signal-to-noise ratio, signal strength, and other information about how well your Wi-Fi LAN is behaving.

If you want to know the details, you can just run a test and see the outcome, as shown in Figure 2.2.

Figure 2.2
This ORiNOCO Client Manager software tells you a lot about your current LAN connection quality.

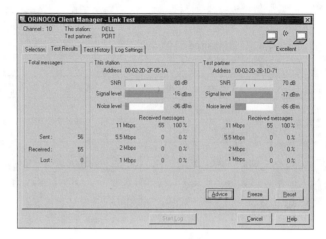

As you can see in Figure 2.2, the connection in this Peer-to-Peer Wi-Fi LAN is described as "excellent." (I named my desktop computer *Dell* and my portable *Port*. That's why those names appear at the top of the report as "This Station" and "Test Partner." If I ran the Client Manager utility from my portable, these names would be reversed, with the Dell desktop described as the "Test Partner.")

Notice, too, in Figure 2.2 that all the messages sent between these computers (111 messages altogether) have been transmitted at the full 11Mbps speed. Any slowness observed in this connection is not the fault of the Wi-Fi LAN itself. There has been no scale back because this signal is so strong and is also uncontaminated by interference. No matter how strong your signal is, your data won't transmit if it must fight high interference pollution—just as you might not hear your friend's remarks at a rock concert, even if your friend is yelling at you.

UNDERSTANDING SNR

The signal strength (or "level") shown in Figure 2.2 is terrific, as is the relatively low noise level. Combine these two measurements and you get the Signal-to-Noise ratio (SNR), which is quite good here—off the chart, actually. If you suspect that a radio station, portable phone, or (rarely) a microwave oven is interfering with your Wi-Fi, take a look at the signal to noise ratio of your communication.

Dealing with Interference

Interference in the Wi-Fi band will cause your Signal to Noise ratio readings to drop below 50%. If this happens, you'll have to take steps. A Wi-Fi LAN unit only transmits data when no other station is transmitting. It's not a free-for-all; it's one-at-a-time communication. Therefore, while there is sufficient interference, your Wi-Fi data is not being transmitted until the interference goes away.

What steps can you take? If you are a real propeller-head, you can track down the source of the interference by whipping out your spectrum analyzer. It will show you what specific frequencies within the Wi-Fi band are causing the interference. Then you can track down the source of the interference based on its frequencies.

You don't carry a pocket spectrum analyzer? Then try this: Run a software utility like that shown in Figure 2.2 on a portable computer, then walk around the building watching the SNR figure. You should be able to notice the source of local interference because the SNR will degrade as you get near the microwave oven or portable phone that's causing the trouble. Or turn the oven or phone on and off, observing the effects on the SNR. Perhaps something as simple as moving the oven to another part of the building, or replacing a portable phone with one using a different band will cure your interference problems.

Obviously, it's not a good idea to install 2.4GHz wireless phones where you want to install a Wi-Fi LAN (which itself also uses 2.4GHz).

Finally, if you install several Wi-Fi access points in the same location, will *they* interfere with each other? Fortunately, no. As you'll see in Chapter 3, Wi-Fi units communicate via several channels, which don't interfere with each other.

INSTALLING A SIMPLE WI-FI NETWORK

It's now time for you to take your hands out of your pockets and get your small, simple Wi-Fi LAN up and working. Remember, if you're interested in building a larger-scale wireless network—or more than say 10 machines or with special requirements—you might want to skip to Chapter 3 "Larger Scale Wi-Fi Setups."

WANT TO BE AN ADMINISTRATOR?

Windows NT and 2000 divide users into various groups, giving them different levels of access to the operating system and hard drive. When you log on with your username/password combination, Windows 2000 looks up your "identity" in its Registry. Part of your identity specifies which group you belong to, which category you fall into—spelling out how much access you have to make changes to the computer's behavior or to files on its hard drive.

You must be logged on to a computer as an Administrator to be able to make a machine running Windows 2000 join a workgroup, and to edit other specifications necessary to build a Wi-Fi LAN. If you don't know how to qualify yourself as an administrator, ask an administrator. It's a chicken and egg problem.

The only way to get Administrator status is to convince an existing Administrator to give you that status. It's exactly like trying to join an exclusive private club. If you're not already in, well…why aren't you? What's wrong with you?

Administrators have the greatest freedom of all classes of computer users to modify the behavior of the operating system, assign passwords, supervise networking, and so on. And they're the only ones who can create new Administrators.

Windows's Help feature is deliberately vague about describing the process of transforming yourself from an ordinary user into an administrator, for the same reason that guards at the Pentagon are vague about how you get into the building.

However, here's a brief description of the steps necessary if you want to upgrade your status to install your Wi-Fi LAN.

When Windows 2000 is installed, there are two default users: guest and administrator. If you installed your home or small office computer, you're probably an administrator already. To find out if you are an administrator, click Start, Settings, Control Panel and then double-click the Users and Passwords icon. If you're not an administrator, you won't even be able to see the Users and Passwords dialog box. Instead, you'll get a rather cold message stating that you're logged on as Molly (or whatever your user name is) and this Molly is simply not a member of the Administrators group.

Even if you are not at the administrator level, it's still likely that an administrator upgraded your status to something higher than *guest* (guest is the lowest of the low). You're probably in the User group, or maybe even the Power User group. But that's just not good enough, sucker.

However, it's worth a try to type Administrator in the User Name field (displayed in that cold message) and leave the password blank. In SOHO environments, administrators sometimes don't bother giving themselves a password, or changing their user name from the default. Then click the OK button. If the Administrator didn't give himself a secret user name and password, you might just find yourself seeing the Users and Passwords dialog box! That's almost like being invited to join Skull and Bones! Now you can follow the steps described next to boost your status to Administrator permanently.

If you cannot get into the Users and Passwords dialog box, you'll have to convince an administrator to adjust your status to administrative-level (all access) permissions. Then you'll be an Administrator at last. Dreams do come true.

If you manage to convince an Administrator that you can be trusted (or somehow get into the Users and Passwords dialog box yourself), here's how to elevate your status from ordinary user to administrator. In the Users and Passwords dialog box you'll see a list of all people who can log on to this machine, and the group that each belongs to (their level of access, such as Debuggers, Power Users, Replicators, Backup Operators, Guests, Users, and so on…don't ask about *replicators* or *debuggers*. It's best not to know too much).

Now click your own user name (Molly or whatever) to select it. Click the Properties button. Click the Group Membership tab. Click the radio button titled Other. Drop open the list and click Administrators. Click the Apply button, and then click the OK button. Click another OK button to close the Users and Passwords dialog box. You'll see a message telling you that you must log off, then back on, for these changes to take effect.

MANUFACTURERS DIFFER

Various vendors differ somewhat in the steps necessary to set up their Wi-Fi hardware, so you do need to try to follow the instructions that came with your equipment.

However, I've found that Wi-Fi equipment setup instructions are often insufficient, sometimes even entirely misleading. In one case, a necessary driver was simply missing from the CD. The manual described the driver and told you where to find it on the CD. The only problem was that when you went to look for the driver, it simply was not on the CD.

In other cases, steps were incorrectly described, or omitted entirely from the setup instructions. For example, the documentation provided by nearly all Wi-Fi companies fails to tell you how to actually get a Wi-Fi Peer-to-Peer LAN actually working. They tell you how to install their hardware, and their software, but then they just *stop*. Or they say something like this in their little booklet:

PREKNOWLEDGE EXPECTATIONS

"The purchaser is expected to know how to work with the Windows operating system, and also how to establish a network within that OS."—from the wireless PC card documentation of a large equipment vendor.

CH

2

Well, maybe you do, and maybe you don't. Lots of people know how to use Windows; very few people have experience setting up networks. If you're setting up a SOHO Wi-Fi installation, it's quite likely that you have no knowledge about networks precisely because you've been working with a few computers in your home or office and they have never been connected into a network. Wi-Fi equipment manufacturers seem to be as yet unaware that the SOHO Wi-Fi market is exploding in popularity.

Few people have set up a network. Few people have established security (password) protocols, dealt with permissions, or managed shares. These are the jobs of a network administrator, and there are lots more of us regular people installing Wi-Fi equipment than there are experienced IS (information systems) professionals.

But we're not complaining. It's precisely this kind of, what shall we call it? Documentation vague-out?—that makes computer books necessary and provides jobs for us computer book authors.

Our struggles locating missing drivers, upgrading firmware, and interpreting less-than-accurate documentation will profit you, dear reader.

So here's the plan. Begin by following the step-by-step directions provided with your Wi-Fi PCM or USB hardware. But when (we won't use the word *if*), your Wi-Fi network fails to work, read the rest of this chapter. We'll tell you what else you need to do. And we're betting that you'll need to do more than the documentation says.

ABOUT THE FOUR-STEP INSTALLATION PROCESS

You follow these four steps to install a typical Wi-Fi client unit (PCM card, PCI adapter or USB client):

1. Connect the client unit physically to the machine (plug it in) In theory, when you plug it in, the Windows 2000 or 98/Me operating system should detect the new peripheral and install the best driver for it—all automatically. That's the *theory*. In practice, you'll probably have to install your driver by hand. All too often, drivers must be installed manually.

2. If, when you plug in your Wi-Fi unit, instructions automatically appear onscreen to help you install the drivers, firmware update (if any) and the utility software—well, good for you. Follow those instructions.

   Windows 98 and Windows 2000 have a feature called Plug and Play (PnP), which is often able to detect that a new peripheral has been attached to the computer. Following detection, PnP can *sometimes* then install the necessary support software (a *driver*, and possibly some additional code libraries). *Sometimes*. PnP also can resolve conflicts with other peripherals, and register the new equipment with the operating system. In our experience, device conflict resolution and registration usually work just fine under PnP. They are handled automatically and correctly. However, driver installation usually doesn't work. If your driver doesn't install, we'll show you what to do later in this chapter.

3. After the driver is installed, Windows can then communicate with the Wi-Fi unit. Your next step is to create a configuration profile for the client hardware. You use utility software provided with your Wi-Fi hardware in this configuration step. You'll define the hardware as a participant in a Peer-to-Peer group, attached to an access point, or used with a residential gateway. In this chapter we'll deal only with the first option, the SOHO Peer-to-Peer setup.

   You also use the manufacturer's utility software to specify a network name, a Wi-Fi channel, and your choice of security (encryption) options. The utility software's signal strength testing is also helpful if you want to choose between several locations for your computers, decide to add an outboard antenna (where best to place it?), need to track down the source of interference, or want to find out how fast your data can transfer from various points in your locale.

4. Finally, you work with the Windows operating system to set up your Peer-to-Peer workgroup, to provide your computer name, to specify the name of the workgroup, and to permit sharing of files and printers (if this is the first time you've created a network to which this computer will belong). You'll find the necessary dialog boxes to complete this step in Control Panel. Windows 98 users double-click the Network icon, then click the Identification tab. Windows 2000 users double-click the System icon, then click the Network Identification tab. There's no particular reason why these two operating systems use different approaches when setting up networking. They just do.

GET THE LATEST VERSION

Because it's often essential information, I'm going to repeat and expand on my earlier warning in case you missed it. Wi-Fi is a cutting-edge technology and many manufacturers are upgrading their utility software, drivers, and firmware quite frequently (two or three times a year!). It's likely, therefore, that the CD enclosed with the Wi-Fi hardware you bought contains perhaps not the latest, best software. I therefore suggest that before you start installing your support software, go to your manufacturer's Web site and look for "software support," "technical support," "downloads," or some similar link. Then check to see whether there is a recent version of software to support your Wi-Fi unit. Here, for example, is the page where you can find the latest Lucent/Agere support software:

`www.orinocowireless.com/template.html?section=m52&envelope=90`

And check out the Cisco page at `www.cisco.com`.

Look up the drivers and utilities based on your operating system—Windows 2000, 98, Me, or whatever—and then based on the product.

If you do download software, be sure to read any README.TXT or README.HTM files that come with the downloaded software. It will likely tell you how to install the software.

DON'T MIX AND MATCH

Drivers and firmware almost always have to work together as a matched pair, and utility software also often must work with these particular, specific versions as well. They must be the same "build" or version, or they will not cooperate. So if you're installing new firmware, you'll probably have to replace your driver as well. *Firmware* is not hardware, nor is it software—it's not hard nor soft, it's in between: *firm*. It means that some hardware (like your access point unit, or USB unit) has a rewritable chip inside. You can download some updated software, run the software, and it seeks out and injects itself into your unit. Firmware makes it possible to update the behavior of hardware, without actually replacing anything physical.

STEP 1: ATTACHING THE HARDWARE

Now plug the USB cable into the USB Wi-Fi unit, then plug the other end of the USB cable into a USB port on your computer. Or if you're adding a PCM card, plug it in. Both USB units and PCM cards feature hot-swapping, so this means that you can leave your computer running while you plug or unplug these devices.

 Hot swapping is not a good idea when working with peripherals that attach to the serial or parallel ports, or other kinds of connections such as plugging into a video card, removing an internal (PCI) card, plugging in an outboard CD burner drive, and so on. In those cases, to prevent possible damage, always turn off the power before plugging or unplugging a device.

As soon as you hot-swap in your new card or USB unit, Windows 2000 or Windows 98 should attempt to detect the new peripheral.

STEP 2: DRIVER INSTALLATION UNDER WINDOWS 98

At this point we'll describe the process for setting up your Wi-Fi Peer-to-Peer network under Windows 98. Then, later in the chapter, we'll describe the setup process under Windows 2000 (which is a bit easier, usually).

CH

2

The following setup description is fairly typical, but your particular equipment may require some variations:

1. If Windows 98 cannot automatically detect your hardware, it will display the message shown in Figure 2.3.

Figure 2.3
Windows 98 is telling you to manually install the driver for your Wi-Fi card or USB client unit.

> **Information**
>
> The driver for your wireless PC Card has not been installed.
> To start the installation of the driver insert your wireless PC Card in your computer.
>
> If the operating system can not find the correct driver, you may have to browse the CD-ROM and point the driver installer to the following folder:
>
> X:\Drivers\Win_98 (where X is your CD ROM drive letter)
>
> OK

2. If Windows 98 has detected your hardware, it will start its Add New Hardware Wizard, as shown in Figure 2.4.

Figure 2.4
This wizard can install the necessary support software for a new peripheral.

> **Add New Hardware Wizard**
>
> This wizard searches for new drivers for:
>
> ORiNOCO USB Client
>
> A device driver is a software program that makes a hardware device work.
>
> < Back   Next >   Cancel

3. If it doesn't automatically start, go ahead and manually start the wizard. Click Start, Settings, Control Panel. Then double-click the Add New Hardware icon in Control Panel.

4. Click Next. You see the dialog box shown in Figure 2.5.

Figure 2.5
Choose to have
Windows search.

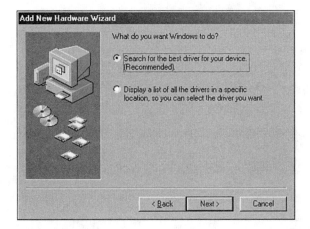

5. Click Next. You see the dialog box shown in Figure 2.6.

Figure 2.6
If you have a CD from
the manufacturer
with the latest, best
software on it, go
ahead and specify
that the CD should be
searched.

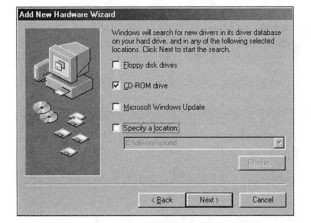

6. Click Next. Windows will search the CD. Often, Windows will search a CD, but will not find what it needs. It is looking for a particular file that ends in the extension .INF (or sometimes .SYS). There may be several subdirectories on the CD, containing different .INF files for different operating systems. Or the .INF file may not be the correct version, or it might be missing.

7. If Windows's search fails to locate what it needs, you'll see the message shown in Figure 2.7.

CH
2

Figure 2.7
Woe is you! The auto-installing process wasn't as *auto* as we hoped it would be.

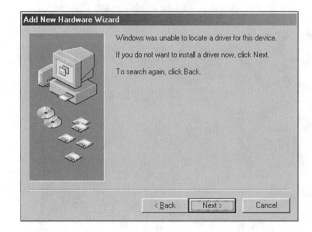

8. Next, click the Back button and return to the dialog box shown in Figure 2.6. This time, click the Specify a location checkbox (see Figure 2.8).

Figure 2.8
Use this option to locate the right .INF file yourself. The wizard has not done its job.

9. Click the Browse button and try to find a subdirectory on your CD that says something like Drivers\Windows98 or some such. Click Next and see whether this time the wizard lives up to its name and finds the .INF file that it needs.

10. If things still don't work—and believe me, they all too often don't—you should now go to the manufacturer's Web site and look for their software/update download/tech help section or whatever they call it. Find, then download, all the files for your equipment

and operating system. Put them into a temporary directory on your hard drive (create a new directory with File, New Folder in Windows Explorer—name it TEMPDRIVER or something). Extract all the files, if necessary, into that temporary directory.

11. Click the Back button again in the wizard to return to the dialog box shown in Figure 2.6. Click the Specify a location checkbox again. Click the Browse button and locate the TEMPDRIVER folder. Do not click the Next button yet.

12. If you have downloaded the latest software from the manufacturer's Web site, it is likely that there will also be new firmware and/or utility software to go along with the new driver. Be sure to install the firmware (usually all you have to do is click the firmware installing .EXE file in Windows Explorer). Also be sure to install the newer version of the utility software as well.

13. Click Next now. This time things should work out for you. You should see the wizard claim that it has found "the best" driver for this device (see Figure 2.9). *As if!* You did it, not the wizard. Anyway, go ahead and click Next so the thing gets installed.

CH

2

Figure 2.9
The wizard says it has found the best driver for your device.

14. If you still cannot get Windows 98 to install the Wi-Fi unit's driver, it's time to get on the phone and call the manufacturer's technical customer service people and tell them your story. Some will respond to your call within minutes, 24 hours a day. Others can put you on hold for a long, long time, and only answer calls during certain periods. Lucent/Agere/ORiNOCO, for one, offers excellent tech help.

If you have now installed your Windows 98 driver, skip down to the section titled "Creating Your Wi-Fi Connection Under Windows 98 or Windows 2000."

STEP 2 CONTINUED: DRIVER INSTALLATION UNDER WINDOWS 2000

The steps that install a driver under Windows 2000 are similar to those you follow under Windows 98, but Windows 2000 is a bit more advanced. It generally requires less of you:

1. After you've plugged in your Wi-Fi units, the Setup Wizard should fire up, declaring that it has detected new Plug-and-Play hardware, as shown in Figure 2.10.

Figure 2.10
Plug and Play displays this message to let you know it's on the case.

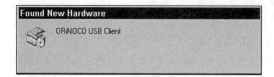

2. If the Setup Wizard doesn't fire up when you plug in your new Wi-Fi client card (or USB unit), choose Start, Settings, Control Panel and double-click the Add/Remove Hardware icon.

3. Click Next and select Add/Troubleshoot.

4. Click Next. Windows 2000 will search for a new device. You may be told that the wizard cannot find the drivers (see Figure 2.11).

Figure 2.11
The wizard might want you to specify where it can find the right driver.

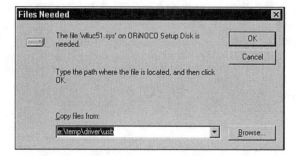

5. If you see the dialog box shown in Figure 2.11, click the Browse button and find the directory where the driver is located on the manufacturer's CD (see Figure 2.12).

6. Try to find a subdirectory on the CD that says something like Drivers\Windows2000 or some such. Click Next and see whether this time the wizard lives up to its name and finds the file that it needs.

7. If things still don't work—and believe me, they all too often don't—you should now go to the manufacturer's Web site and look for their software/update download/tech help section or whatever they call it.

Find, then download, the latest set of files for your equipment (card, USB or access port hardware) and your operating system (Windows 2000 in this case). Put these files into a temporary directory on your hard drive (create a new directory with File, New Folder in Windows Explorer—name it TEMPDRIVER or something). Extract all the files, if necessary, into that temporary directory (if they are in a ZIP format, use the WinZip utility, which can be downloaded from the Internet at `www.winzip.com/`).

Figure 2.12
You can usually browse the manufacturer's CD to find the needed file.

8. After you've downloaded the files from the manufacturer, and unzipped them, click the Back button again in the wizard to return to the previous page. Click the Browse button and locate your new TEMPDRIVER folder. Do not click the Next button yet.

9. If you have downloaded the latest software from the manufacturer's Web site, it is likely that there will also be new firmware and/or utility software to go along with the new driver. (Be sure to double-click any README files that were downloaded for information.) Install any firmware (usually all you have to do is click the firmware installing .EXE file in Windows Explorer) *before* installing the driver. Also be sure to install the newer version of the utility software—if it was downloaded—as well. Then click the Next button in the wizard to install the driver. (If all this fails to install your driver, contact the manufacturer's technical support staff.)

DIGITAL SIGNATURES

If you're told that a digital signature is missing during the driver installation process, you can either take cover immediately, or, if you're daring like me, click Yes and continue the installation (see Figure 2.13).

Figure 2.13
This idea of digital signatures was a noble experiment that really didn't catch on. It was an attempt to protect us from viruses, but it has some flaws.

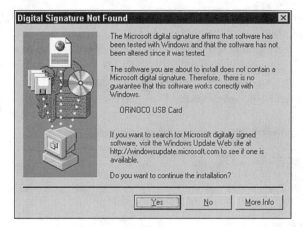

STEP 3: USING UTILITY SOFTWARE TO DEFINE A WI-FI CONNECTION UNDER WINDOWS 98 OR WINDOWS 2000

Once the driver is installed, it's time to specify some properties of your Wi-Fi card or USB unit. This process will be described for both Windows 98 and Windows 2000 in this section.

You now must choose some specifications and behaviors for your Wi-Fi LAN cards (or USB units). The following steps are typical, but the specifics in the next examples are from the Lucent ORiNOCO utility software. (Following this section, we'll describe the final steps you take—setting up a Peer-to-Peer network, activating Network Neighborhood and Sharing—which are *not* manufacturer-dependent steps.)

1. Run the utility software that came with your Wi-Fi unit, and that you installed during the driver installation process described earlier in this chapter.

   The utility software will assist you in specifying various options such as TCP/IP settings, profiles, channel numbers, network type (Peer-to-Peer, Access Point or others), encryption options, and so on.

   If you don't know how to activate this software to complete this part of setting up your Wi-Fi LAN, check the manual that came with your Wi-Fi hardware, or call their technical support people.

2. When you run the ORiNOCO Client Manager utility program, select Actions, Add/Edit Configuration Profile to bring up the Add/Edit Configuration Profile dialog box (see Figure 2.14). This dialog box (or your manufacturer's equivalent) might automatically appear after the driver is successfully installed.

Figure 2.14
You specify how your Wi-Fi unit should behave in this dialog box.

3. Click the Add button; you see the dialog box shown in Figure 2.15 where you give this profile a name, and choose Peer-to-Peer. You can set up several "profiles" if you want. Use any profile name you want, but your choice of Network Type must match this same choice on other computers you want to communicate with.

Figure 2.15
Choose the Peer-to-Peer Network Type.

4. Click Next. You now see the dialog box shown in Figure 2.16.

5. Pay special attention to this step: Give your network a name, such as *Orinoco*, and choose a channel number.

Figure 2.16
These two
specifications are
crucial.

 Note

All computers participating in this Peer-to-Peer workgroup must use the same network name and channel number. Also, the network name is case sensitive: Orinoco will not work with orinoco—they do not match. Many people don't ensure that the name and channel match, and they wonder why they cannot see the other computer(s) on their Wi-Fi LAN.

Tip

The term *Network Name* is synonymous with the terms *SSID, network ID,* and *workgroup name.*

6. Click Next and leave the data security option turned off. We'll deal with the many interesting facets of Wi-Fi security in Chapter 8, "Security and Encryption." However, if you fear that your personal life, or your small business, is so wildly entertaining or precious that outsiders are lurking around just waiting for your Wi-Fi LAN to turn on so they can eavesdrop, then select Enable Data Security. Be sure, though, that you also select this option when setting up the other computers in this same workgroup, or they will not see each other and no communication will take place.

7. Click Next twice. Ignore the TCP/IP Behavior option.

8. Click Finish.

9. Click OK to close the dialog box.

⚠ *Because so many phone calls to Wi-Fi tech service people result from this particular error, I'm going to repeat this warning. You are setting up two (or more) machines that must be able to join together in the same workgroup LAN (peer-to-peer network). They must share four qualities that were defined in this section:*

- *The same Network Type (peer-to-peer).*

- *The same Network Name. (Choose whatever you want, but ensure that all machines in this same LAN use this same Network Name, and that the names match exactly in terms of capitalization: Port does not match port).*

- The same Channel (again, whatever channel you want, but make it the same for all).
- The same data security. (Either no data security, or if turned on, the same key must be used and must be the correct one. See Chapter 8.)

Tip

I've just warned you that you must ensure a match between your network type, SSID name, channel number, encryption settings, or your Wi-Fi units cannot communicate in a peer-to-peer setup. You might wonder, then, how someone can wander into a Starbucks, flip open his laptop, and immediately see his computer connect via Wi-Fi to the Internet. Or, how can someone walk through a large office (roaming, as it's called) from one Wi-Fi access point to another, yet remain connected even though the channel numbers and other settings are different for each access point?

The answer to this mystery is the access point. An access point can, in effect, say: "I detect a laptop Wi-Fi PCM card in my vicinity. If you want to make a connection to me, set your channel to Any, your SSID to 2402s3, and your network type to access point." If your PCM card isn't set to prohibit this communication, it will follow orders and the connection will be made. Encryption, however, in public Wi-Fi LANs like Starbucks, must be turned off in the portable (and also the access point).

CH
2

STEP 4: SETTING UP A PEER-TO-PEER NETWORK

Once the Wi-Fi card or USB unit properties have been specified, it's finally time to take the final step in getting your Wi-Fi Peer-to-Peer network up and running. You must now tell Windows that it is connected to a network, and that, yes, you do want it to share its files and peripherals with the other computer on that network.

A peer-to-peer network is small; two computers or fewer. It also doesn't include some of the heavy-duty security often employed in larger client/server networks. Peer-to-peer networking has no *server* machine—no somewhat more powerful computer that serves as a storage, routing, and sometimes a processing center for a group of less capable machines (the clients) dependent on its services.

Instead, in a peer-to-peer setup, the computers are by definition *peers*, equals (or roughly equals, anyway). There's no central server through which communications between clients must flow.

When computers are joined into a local area peer network, you can then right-click on a folder (or drive) in Windows Explorer and choose Sharing from the Context menu to permit other peer machines to access this folder and its contents. Likewise, printers, CD-ROM units, and other peripherals can be shared.

When you attach a network adapter (such as a Wi-Fi unit) to a machine, Windows automatically creates the basis of a LAN for you. Thereafter, each time you start a computer with a network adapter running, the associated LAN is automatically started.

PROTOCOLS

A basic LAN, though, is only the beginning. *You* have to install some network protocols. TCP/IP is automatically installed by default, and that's probably the best protocol for you to use with your Wi-Fi units. To see which protocols are installed on your computer, follow these steps:

1. In Windows 2000, click Start, Settings, Network and Dialup Connections. Then right-click the LAN and choose Properties. You'll see a dialog box like the one shown in Figure 2.17.

Figure 2.17
The Windows 2000
Protocols dialog box.

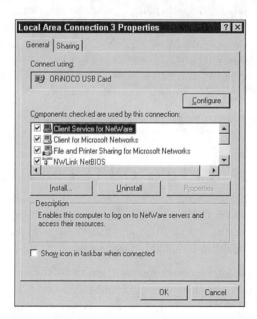

Or in Windows 98, click Start, Settings, Control Panel, Network, and you'll see the Network dialog box shown in Figure 2.18.

2. Now click the TCP/IP protocol listed for your Wi-Fi unit in the dialog box shown in Figure 2.18. This selects your unit.

3. Then click the Properties button shown in Figure 2.18 to get to the actual settings for this protocol (see Figure 2.19).

Figure 2.18
The Windows 98
Network dialog box.

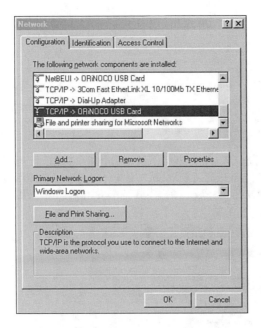

Figure 2.19
Here is where you
can give your Wi-Fi
connection an address
in Windows 98.

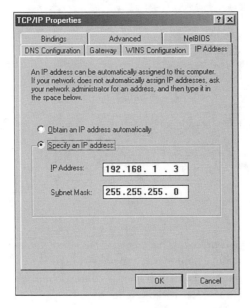

CH
2

SPECIFYING AN IP ADDRESS

If one of your computers connected to your Wi-Fi LAN is using Windows 98, you may
need to assign IP addresses. (If they are both Windows 2000 computers, you can skip this
step—the IP address can be assigned automatically.)

The IP addresses must differ, but only slightly. Give one computer this address:

IP: 192.168.1.3

Subnet: 255.255.255.0

And give the other computer this address:

IP: 192.168.1.2

Subnet: 255.255.255.0

You get to this dialog box in Windows 2000 by locating the Internet Protocol (TCP/IP) in the list shown in Figure 2.17, clicking that entry in the list to select it, and then clicking the Properties button. Now you'll see the dialog box shown in Figure 2.20.

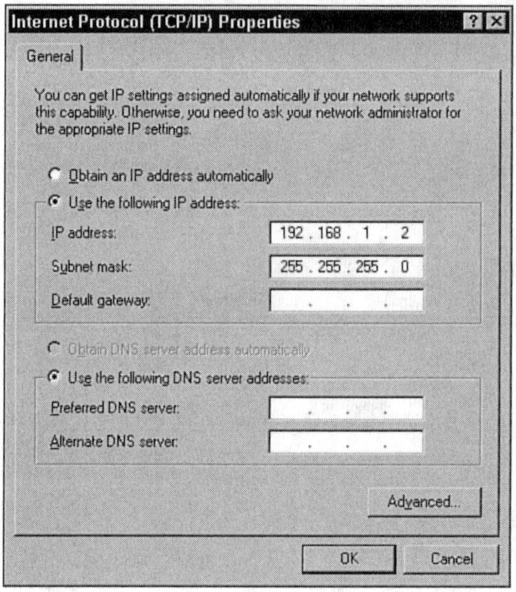

Figure 2.20
Here is where you can give your Wi-Fi connection an *address* in Windows 2000.

JOINING A WORKGROUP

Recall that after the connection protocols have been established, you need to give your computer a unique name (each machine that is a member of the Wi-Fi LAN must have its own unique name). The computer's name will identify this machine when other computers connected to this LAN look in the Network Neighborhood.

You also create a workgroup by specifying a workgroup name. It can be up to 15 characters long, but cannot be the same name as the computer name. It cannot contain any of the following characters:

; : " < > * + = \ | ? ,

THE WINDOWS 2000 VERSION

In Windows 2000, follow these steps:

1. Click Start, Control Panel, and then double-click the System icon in Control Panel.
2. Click the Network Identification tab (see Figure 2.21).

Figure 2.21
Use this dialog box to identify (or rename) your computer, and to join a workgroup.

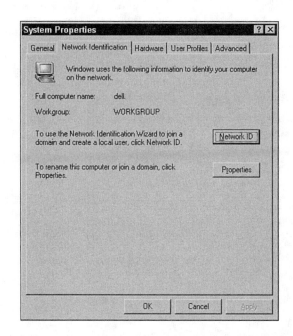

CH

2

3. Click the Properties button shown in Figure 2.21, and you'll see the page shown in Figure 2.22.

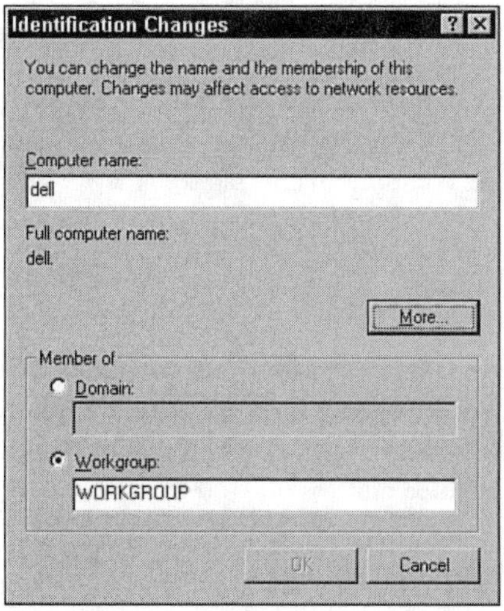

Figure 2.22
The name you gave your computer when you installed your operating system appears here, but you can change it if you want (Windows 2000 version).

4. Click the Workgroup radio button shown in Figure 2.22, and then type in a name. I used the name *Workgroup*, but it can be any name you want. However, make sure that all computers in this workgroup use this same name. Otherwise, your Wi-Fi LAN will fail.

THE WINDOWS 98 VERSION

To accomplish the same thing in Windows 98, follow these steps:

1. Click Start, Settings, Control Panel, Network, and you'll see the Network dialog box shown in Figure 2.23.

Figure 2.23
Rename your computer here, if you want, and join the workgroup (Windows 98 version).

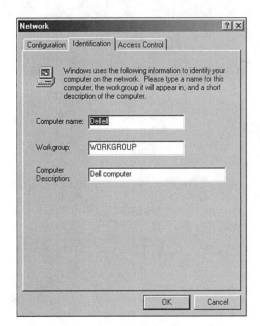

2. Notice that the machine settings shown in Figure 2.23 include a different name from the one shown in Figure 2.22, but the same workgroup name. That way, they can communicate over a Wi-Fi LAN. They would fail to communicate if they had different workgroup names, or the same computer name.

SHARING: IT'S A GOOD THING

It's time to share your drives, folders, and files with other computers that are part of your workgroup. In an office context, you likely will agree to share files that you and co-workers need to work on together. However, there might also be files you want to keep private and refuse to share. Your personal annotated address book, for instance.

This section describes how to share (and also how to refuse to share). When you join a network, some interesting new issues confront you. Do you want everyone else to see everything on your computer's hard drive? Probably not. For one thing, your Cookies, Internet cache, and Favorites folders tell a great deal about you. People looking through those folders can probably learn a lot more about your personality than if they looked at your bookshelves and magazine collections at your home. And there are other places on your hard drive that you might prefer to keep personal.

Your hard drive's contents are not, by default, shared. You must explicitly specify that they should be shared (and on a Windows 2000 machine, you must be an Administrator to create shares). Note though that anyone with Administrator status can read all your files, even if you specifically designate those files as not shared.

You can specify the sharing options for individual files by right-clicking the filename in Windows Explorer, then choosing Properties and clicking the Security tab in the Properties dialog box. To specify the sharing options for folders, hard drives, printers, CD drives, and other peripherals, right-click their name in Windows Explorer, then choose Sharing from the Context menu. Step-by-step instructions are provided in a moment.

Tip

There are additional security measures you can take in Windows 2000 to guard your special files and folders, including user and group accounts, Group Policy, auditing, and user rights. Also, if you use the NTFS hard drive technology, you can set file and folder permissions and even encrypt files and folders. This chapter covers only the simple sharing permissions, plus read-only and full modification options. Chapter 8 tackles heavy-duty security for people who have something really valuable to guard, or at least think they do. I once worked for a very small publishing company and for a while we went through a paranoid phase. We shredded lots of documents that absolutely nobody was remotely interested in, or would have benefited from in any way.

If you don't see them listed, don't panic. We'll list some tricks you can try to get things working later in this chapter in the section "Testing Your Connection."

THE WINDOWS 98 VERSION

To share a whole drive with other machines in your Wi-Fi LAN, right-click the drive in Windows Explorer. Choose Sharing from the Context menu. You'll see the dialog box shown in Figure 2.24.

If you do share an entire drive, you can still use Windows Explorer to exclude particular directories or files from your generous sharing. Just right-click the name of the directory or file you want to keep private, and then click Sharing in the Context menu and choose Not Shared.

Figure 2.24
Give this C: drive a name (to identify it on the network) and also define the *degree* of sharing (the "access type").

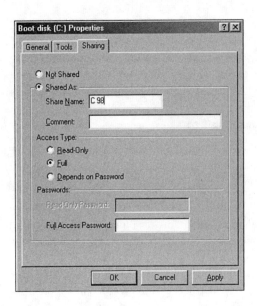

This tactic will not prevent Administrators from getting to your secret directories or files (to hide things from an Administrator, you'll have to resort to encryption, as described in Chapter 8). However, this tactic will keep out the rabble, people with less-than-Administrator status. Ordinary people when they try to read one of your "not shared" files, will get an error message stating `The document name or path is not valid. Try these suggestions. Check the file permissions for the document or drive...`

Under access type, either let outsiders read-only (they cannot modify the files), have full access, or make this distinction depend on their password.

Now you want to flip the general sharing switch. Click Start, Settings, Control Panel, Network. Click the Configuration tab and click the File and Print Sharing button. You'll see the dialog box shown in Figure 2.25.

Figure 2.25
Let outsiders have general access to your files and any printer attached to your machine.

THE WINDOWS 2000 VERSION

To share a whole drive with other machines in your Wi-Fi LAN, right-click the drive in Windows Explorer. Choose Sharing from the Context menu. You'll see the dialog box shown in Figure 2.26.

Figure 2.26
This is the Windows 2000 version of the sharing dialog box.

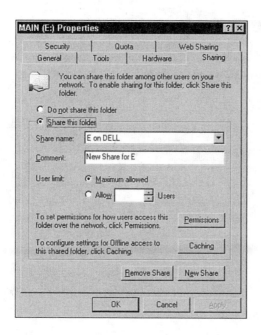

Give your drive a name and select the Share This Folder radio button (it says Folder, but it means drive).

If you do share an entire drive, you can still use Windows Explorer to exclude particular directories or files from your generous sharing. Just right-click the name of the directory you want to keep private, then click Sharing in the Context menu and choose Do Not Share this Folder. To hide a file, right-click its name, choose Properties, and then click the Security tab in the Properties dialog box.

 This tactic will not prevent Administrators from getting to your secret directories or files (to hide things from an Administrator, you'll have to resort to encryption, as described in Chapter 8). However, this tactic will keep out the rabble, people with less-than-Administrator status. Ordinary people—when they try to read one of your "not shared" files—will get an error message stating "The document name or path is not valid. Try these suggestions. Check the file permissions for the document or drive."

Click the Permissions button and you'll see the dialog box shown in Figure 2.27.

Under access type, either let outsiders read-only (they cannot modify the files), have full access, or make this distinction depend on their password.

CH
2

Figure 2.27
Set the access level in this dialog box.

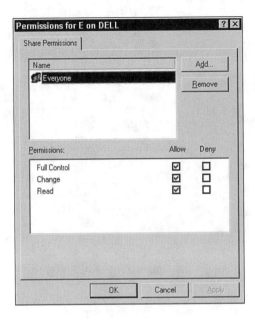

Now permit printer sharing. In Internet Explorer click My Network Places, Entire Network, Microsoft Windows Network, WorkGroup (or whatever name you gave your workgroup), Dell (or the name of your computer, to which a printer is attached), Printers.

You now see the printer or printers attached to this computer listed (see Figure 2.28).

PROVIDING PRINTER PERMISSION

Figure 2.28
Here's where you can permit printer sharing in Windows 2000.

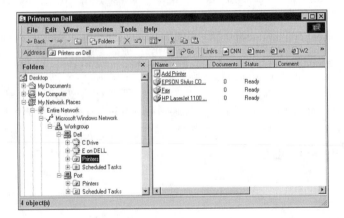

Now right-click the name of a printer and choose Sharing (or Properties, Sharing). You'll see the dialog box displayed in Figure 2.29.

Figure 2.29
This printer has not been specified as "sharing" so others on your Wi-Fi LAN cannot use it.

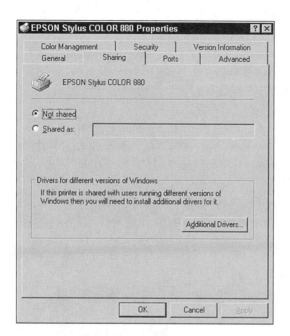

Click the Shared As radio button (the default name of the printer will now appear in the text field next to the radio button). Click Apply, and then OK to close the dialog box.

Now outsiders can use this printer while they are working in Word or some other program, and try to print (choose File, Print).

The outsiders will see a dialog box, if no printer is attached to their remote machine. They can go ahead and choose to "install" the printer on their computer (this is a virtual install—they're really working across the Wi-Fi LAN). The Add Printer Wizard appears. They then must follow the instructions to locate a Network Printer and click Next to browse your network. The network will be searched for a printer. They should now see the printer you "shared" listed under the name of your computer.

They should click it to select it, and then click Next. The Add Printer Wizard will gather some information (this might take a while—don't necessarily blame Wi-Fi!). Then they are asked whether they want this to be the default printer for this computer. It's up to them. Next they click Finish to close the wizard. Now they have the ability to print documents over the air from your remote machine to the printer attached to the local machine.

Tip

Follow this same basic process to provide access to other peripherals attached to computers on the Wi-Fi LAN, such as Zip drives and so on. However, scanners and some other peripherals can require proprietary setups that prevent their use across a network. Even if you install the proprietary drivers and such on each of your networked computers, they might not work unless a machine is *directly* connected to the scanner. Printers and hard drives, fortunately, do not suffer from this problem.

TESTING YOUR CONNECTION

How do you know whether your two Wi-Fi "connected" computers are actually talking to each other and the LAN is operational? Turn on both computers. Go to one of the machines, which we'll call the "local" computer. Run Windows Explorer in the local computer. Now see whether you can view the hard drive contents of the remote machine.

You'll have to "drill down" a little: Open My Network Places in Windows 2000 Explorer, then under that open Entire Network, Microsoft Windows Network, Workgroup (or whatever name your Peer-to-Peer network has). The Windows 98 version is Network Neigborhood, Entire Network, Workgroup.

Do you now see the names of both your local computer and the remote computer listed? Can you double-click the name of the remote computer and see some of its files listed?

If the dialog box shown in Figure 2.30 appears, you will have to enter a user name and password.

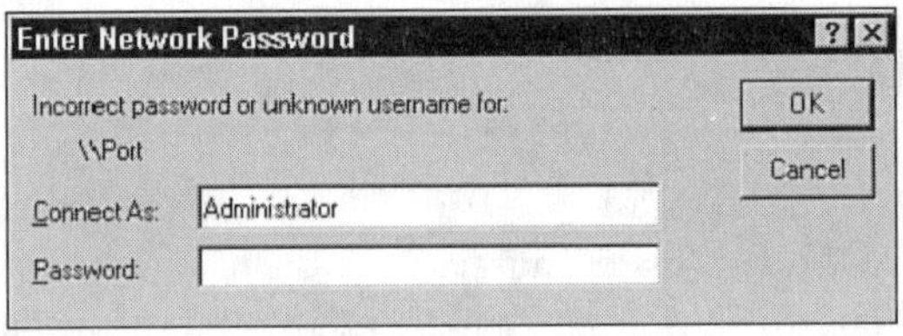

Figure 2.30
This user name/password dialog box is one line of defense in Wi-Fi LAN security.

In the Connect As field, you can type either the name you use when Windows first runs, or you might be able to use Administrator. Many people, particularly in friendly home environments, have no need for a password, so when they turn on the computer the password field is blank. They've never used a password. If you do have a password, however, you'll need to type it in. When you connect to a remote machine over a network, you are, in a sense, signing on to that computer.

SUCCESS...

If your Wi-Fi LAN is working correctly, you should see something like the left pane in Figure 2.31 (in Windows 2000). The remote computer's shared drives, directories, files and peripherals are now available to the connected computer(s) on the Wi-Fi LAN. The Windows 98 version is shown in Figure 2.32.

Figure 2.31
Here's the remote computer (named *Port* in my case—for *portable*) displaying its C: drive, its printers, and its Scheduled Tasks.

Figure 2.32
Windows 98 uses this slightly different tree.

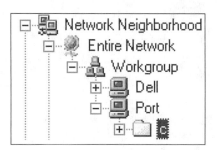

Tip

Some people using Windows Explorer to see a hard drive directory on a Wi-Fi LAN connected computer think it takes "a long time" to see the hard drive's contents listed. This slowness isn't the fault of the Wi-Fi connection. The hard drive speed, the size of the hard drive, and other factors local to the queried machine cause this slow perceived response. Also, directory lists are cached. Cached? This is a trick that makes accessing frequently used data faster. When you first start Windows running on a computer, and first fire up Windows Explorer to see the hard drive, the computer takes a relatively long time to read your hard drive's contents and display the results (this is especially noticeable on really large hard drives, such as 40Gb). However, after the drive's contents are read, the results are then saved in a cache so when you subsequently ask for a hard drive list, the results slap up onscreen really fast. A remote networked computer demonstrates this same slow first look behavior.

Contents of drives viewed through Network Neighborhood are not mapped. These contents only cache easily if both computers are using the same operating system, such as Windows 2000. Put another way, you will not get a quick directory listing the second time you view that directory (refresh it) if you have Windows Me on your notebook and Windows 2000 on your desktop machine. It takes just as long every time to load the information in the directories on the Me machine. However, getting a refreshed

> view of a directory when two computers are using Windows 2000 does not take any time at all. Perhaps the biggest slowdown when viewing another computer's folders is when you have a firewall running. In that case, the display is always slow, and is not cached.

... OR FAILURE

If you don't see the remote computer, you might instead see a dialog box informing you that the remote computer isn't available (see Figure 2.33).

Figure 2.33
This is one of several possible error messages you might see when a Wi-Fi LAN connection fails.

There are several other error dialog boxes that might appear instead of the one shown in Figure 2.33 (that one can be caused by something as simple as the remote computer's power being off).

Or you might find that Windows Explorer itself comes down with a raging fever and odd things start happening onscreen, like the dreaded spluttering boxes phenomenon that you can see in Figure 2.34.

Figure 2.34
The only cure for this is to restart Windows.

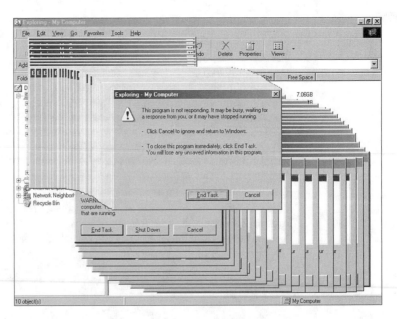

WHAT TO DO IF ALL ELSE FAILS

So, you've carefully followed the setup instructions in your Wi-Fi units' manuals, you've read through this chapter, and you've tried everything you can think of—but your Wi-Fi LAN still isn't operating? Join the club.

We've had two decades now for PCs to accumulate inconsistencies between semi-compatible peripherals, mismatched drivers, IRQ conflicts, and all kinds of other variables. Add to that irregularities across operating systems, legacy dynamic link library clashes, and protocols performing jobs they were never intended to perform. It's a wonder that PCs work as well as they do.

CH
2

You've heard about the bet where someone agrees to double the number of pennies on each square of a checkerboard. By the end, they have a massive fortune. Well, the number of possible permutations of hardware and software on a typical PC is—if not in the billions—at least beyond most people's patience.

Fortunately, you don't have to try all possible permutations. Many problems have been solved. USB plugs only fit into USB ports; Plug and Play *does* solve several problems that used to plague computer users; and most software has become less unstable over the years.

Here are some additional things to try that might get your Wi-Fi LAN working:

- Move the two computers close to each other, to see whether distance or obstacles, is preventing a good connection.
- Check the LED lights on the Wi-Fi units to see whether they are behaving as the manual says they should. They can provide a clue as to what is malfunctioning.
- Restart both computers (drivers, the Windows Registry, and other software sometimes needs this to work properly after first being installed).
- Ensure that the utility software that came with your Wi-Fi units is installed and working correctly. Click Start, Programs, the name of your manufacturer. Or look in Control Panel for a new icon, probably named Wireless Network or similar.
- Unplug, then plug back in, your Wi-Fi units. This reseating is sometimes necessary. Even after the Wi-Fi LAN has been working fine for weeks, you might need to reseat the units from time to time.
- Double-check that the following are the same in both the local and remote computers on the Wi-Fi LAN—Network Type is set to Peer-to-Peer; same Workgroup Name (remember, this name is case sensitive); same Channel number; same security settings. How to check these items is described in this chapter.
- Double-check that the TCP/IP addresses are different in both the local and remote computers on the Wi-Fi LAN. If a Windows 98/Me computer is involved, you may need to specify TCP/IP addresses. These addresses must differ, but be close to each other. See the section titled "Specifying an IP Address" in this chapter.
- Double-check that the computer names you've given your remote and local computers are different. Also ensure that the workgroup names are not the same as the computer names.

- Try adding or removing NetBEUI and IPX/SPX protocols (also called *components*) using the dialog box shown in Figure 2.17 (Windows 2000) or Figure 2.18 (in Windows 98, click the Properties button after selecting the Wi-Fi unit in the list).

- Check to see whether the Wi-Fi units are installed correctly and the computer sees, and accepts, their presence. In Windows 2000, right-click the My Computer icon on your desktop, then choose Properties and click the Hardware tab. Click the Device Manager button. In Windows 98, right-click the My Computer icon on your desktop, then choose Properties and click the Device Manager tab. Now look at the list of hardware attached to your machine. Find the Wi-Fi unit. If you see a yellow exclamation point symbol next to your unit's name, there is likely a conflict of resources between your unit and an already installed peripheral.

  If so, go back to the beginning and try again: In the Control Panel, use the software (add/remove) utility to uninstall the Wi-Fi unit's driver and utility software from your computer. Then use Control Panel's hardware (add/remove) utility to uninstall the Wi-Fi unit itself. Unplug the Wi-Fi unit. Now follow the steps in your manual (or in this chapter) to reinstall your unit. Hope that this time when you plug, it plays.

- Ensure that your USB controller is enabled in your computer's BIOS. This is fairly heavy-duty stuff, so you'll want to consult with your computer's tech help people when looking at the BIOS settings.

- Here's a classic one: Be sure that everything is plugged in physically, and that both computers are turned on. Did you hear about the young man calling the tech help line and saying "I can see the CD sitting there, but my computer isn't using it!" The tech says: "You can see it? Did you close the door?" He hears footsteps walking across the young man's room, and the door slams shut.

- Check the Troubleshooting section in your unit's manual.

- Read the FAQ documentation at your manufacturer's Web site.

- Call your manufacturer's tech help line.

Larger Scale Wi-Fi Setups

In this chapter

In Chapter 2, "Setting Up Your Personal Wireless Network," you set up a peer-to-peer Wi-Fi network by merely plugging PCM cards into portables, or adding PCM/PCI cards or USB units to your computers. This system works well where a network is relatively small. There is no server, nor are there any Wi-Fi access point units.

A larger Wi-Fi system involves more than those little PCM cards. You must also install *access point units*. These units typically weigh about one pound and are the size of an ordinary paperback book (see Figure 3.1). Access point units are designed to interface between a wired network, or an Internet connection, or both, and client computers using Wi-Fi cards (PCM or USB equipment). A single access point can service several clients—depending on how close they are to the access point and other considerations.

Figure 3.1
Access point units are about the size of a paperback book, but they pack plenty of power. They're little radio stations.

Tip

A little terminology. You may hear the terms *ad-hoc mode* and *infrastructure mode* in reference to Wi-Fi setups. These terms reflect the distinction between the topics covered in Chapters 2 and 3 in this book. Ad-hoc Wi-Fi installations are small—typically found in a home or small office. They service only a handful of computers, and are also known as *peer-to-peer* networks. Only PCM cards are used in an ad-hoc installation (no access point units). In effect, there are only clients talking to other clients—there is no central "server" nor, usually, is a wired network involved.

By contrast, infrastructure mode describes large Wi-Fi installations (ranging anywhere from, say, an office with ten employees up to a Wi-Fi LAN as big as a university campus). The client PCM cards don't communicate directly with each other; instead, they communicate via access point units. And those access points in turn are (usually) attached to a 10 or 100Mbps ethernet enterprise network. In this way, the clients are connected wirelessly to a wire network and all its elements—including whatever Internet, printer, and other features the network offers. In an all-Wi-Fi infrastructure installation, an ethernet enterprise network is, of course, not involved.

To install Wi-Fi in a larger office or campus, you will need to address several issues that were not covered in Chapter 2. For example, you may need to use antennas, and you are probably adding Wi-Fi to an existing wire network. You might even want to extend your Wi-Fi coverage so that more than one building is part of a greater Wi-Fi *MAN*, or metropolitan area network.

CH
3

THE NEED TO PLAN: BEFORE THE SITE SURVEY

No matter how large your installation, your single most important planning tool is a site survey. But before actually conducting the survey, here are some questions you should ask yourself first. The answers you provide to these questions can impact how you conduct your site survey, and also the final installation and maintenance budgets. And if you outsource your site survey, your answers to these questions will be important to the specialist who conducts the survey:

- Is a Wi-Fi installation necessary?
- Does the current wire network need to be expanded?
- If you have no current network, will you want to combine a wired network with a Wi-Fi component? (Today's wire networks can offer speed and security not yet possible with Wi-Fi equipment.)
- Is the mobility that Wi-Fi offers an important issue for your organization? Do you really need mobility at all? Can all your Wi-Fi units be fixed, desktop units?
- How much security do you need?
- What possible sources of interference are located in your building?
- If your users will be highly mobile, figure out the battery requirements that may require increasing your overall budget.
- What purposes will your employees use Wi-Fi for?
- Estimate the maximum number of people who will be actively transferring data in each area of your building. The more people simultaneously using a given cell (an access point servicing multiple users), the slower the data throughput.

You can. increase throughput in a crowded area by placing multiple access points at the same place within your building, then tuning them to different channels. Each additional access point unit that you place next to the original access point adds an additional potential 11Mbps (actual around 4) bandwidth. Any given client will not see this increase in throughput, because each client communicates with only one access point at a time. However, the aggregate group of clients will experience faster communication when multiple access points are situated in the same location.

■ The throughput needs of a graphic design company are high because graphic files are large. A company that merely exchanges text messages would experience a much lower throughput. A video studio manages huge amounts of data. How bulky is the data you exchange?

■ Scalability: Do you expect to need to expand your Wi-Fi LAN? If so, how much? From building to building? Will it be part of a WAN? (Wide Area Networks span geographically separated sites using either local and long-distance transmission methods.)

■ How much can you afford to spend?

■ Who will administer the LAN?

■ List any special requirements that must be satisfied at your site: outdoor Wi-Fi coverage? Dead zones (where no coverage is needed, such as restrooms)?

■ Having read product reviews on the Internet, which Wi-Fi vendor best suits your needs? If possible, try to purchase or lease all your Wi-Fi equipment from a single vendor. The reason? Some vendors offer special features unique to their equipment, but some of those features may not be usable unless you use only their equipment. Examples of special features include performance boosts, specialized utility software, and so on. If you must mix and match Wi-Fi equipment from different vendors, be sure that the hardware has a Wi-Fi certification of interoperability.

After you've answered these questions, and decided that a Wi-Fi installation is practical, it's time to do a site survey.

Don't forget to assess the utility software that comes with your Wi-Fi hardware, to ensure that you are getting good testing and maintenance features. In our experience, the support software that comes with Wi-Fi equipment varies considerably in quality from vendor to vendor. The software should provide you with good statistics on the status of your links. A logging capability can be useful (to record signal-to-noise and signal strength performance over, say, a 24-hour period). Reviewing a log that reveals extreme noise spikes when the office opens, during coffee breaks, and lunch points to a microwave oven as a source of interference, for example. The software should also make it easy for you to view and adjust configuration settings such as encryption keys, channels and SSIDs, as you can see in Figure 3.2.

Finally, it can also be useful to have software that supports multiple "profiles." This is a convenience for people who must use, say, encryption when communicating with your Wi-Fi LAN, but want to be able to walk into Starbucks and quickly hook up to a public Wi-Fi broadcast in the coffee shop. Instead of having to go through several steps to reconfigure their encryption settings (turning them off, for instance, in Starbucks), they can merely quickly switch profiles.

Figure 3.2
The Agere/ORiNOCO hardware boasts this effective, full-featured support software.

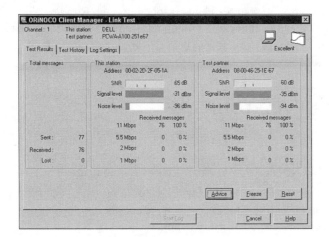

CH
3

CONDUCT A SITE SURVEY

If you're a network administrator in charge of installing a Wi-Fi system, you will first want to conduct a site survey to determine where to put access points, and how many you are likely to need.

A site survey is a practical, real-world series of tests using Wi-Fi equipment, not a theoretical guess based on inflated broadcast-range claims. Under optimal conditions—a room with no obstacles and high ceilings so you can mount the access points high—you might get up to 150 feet range. In an ordinary room—with furniture, walled offices, and such—you might get 75 feet.

Your access point manufacturer may specify a range of 300 feet!

However, immediately after mentioning a range, most manufacturers also admit that this figure is only possible when there are *no obstacles*, and that the transmission distance you will actually achieve *depends on the environment*. Translation: Unless you are setting up your LAN on the airless plains of Mars, expect shorter transmission ranges. Sometimes *much* shorter.

For example, if your school or corporation has a library, you will doubtless discover that you need more access points in the library than in ordinary classrooms or offices. Large quantities of books soak up radio signals fast.

Many companies find it best to outsource the site survey—hiring a professional consultant to draw up a site plan, provide a budget, establish a schedule, estimate scalability, and otherwise design and implement a Wi-Fi installation.

Most businesses have unique requirements. Not only are the various obstacles and interference patterns different, the uses to which a Wi-Fi LAN will be put vary considerably. A factory may require highly mobile inventory control personnel. A warehouse may require similar roaming freedom for a similar inventory control process, but the building might be better for radio propagation. If your warehouse is one big room with few obstructions above four feet high, that's good. If, though, the warehouse contains many tall metal shelves (like those in Sam's Club or Cosco), you're facing a formidable challenge if you're installing full-coverage Wi-Fi.

DOING A SURVEY YOURSELF

If you decide to conduct a site survey yourself, here are the steps you'll want to take:

1. Establish a need. Talk with the people in your organization to find out how many of them would benefit from Wi-Fi's freedom of movement.

2. Draw a diagram of your workplace (or dig out blueprints) and see if you need to cover the entire building, or whether there are areas where computer connectivity would be of little benefit—such as the men's room.

3. Using the drawing, mark the fixed locations of people who will use the Wi-Fi LAN, and also likely mobile locations (such as conference rooms) that will need coverage as well.

   Be aware that there are two distinct types of mobility requirements and your planning should reflect this distinction:

   - *Fixed portability* describes an installation where there are zones that users will likely want to connect to the network, but other areas that no one is likely to need connectivity. For instance, people will likely need to connect in the meeting rooms in your office. But if there is a long empty hallway, or a cold basement, people might carry their portables *through* these areas, but would never actually want to connect to the Wi-Fi LAN there. Also, it might be that your office has one meeting room that is rarely used. In that case, you could make it easy to quickly place an access point unit in this room, but only actually place an access point in there on the few days when this room is used. A similar situation involves a room only used seasonally by temp employees.

   - *Frequent roamers* describes a different kind of Wi-Fi user. They may need continuous connection to your network, and their job may take them everywhere within a building. Examples of this kind of work are inventory takers in warehouses, nurses in a hospital, and so on.

4. Now get scientific and switch from deductive to inductive thinking: Roll up your sleeves and install a Wi-Fi card in a portable computer. Purchase an access point unit. (Use the same Wi-Fi hardware that you intend to use for your final installation. Built-in antennas and other factors vary from one manufacturer to another.) Go throughout your premises, putting the access point in various locations, then walking around with the portable to see the actual range of usable transmission. Consider the roaming patterns likely to take place as people move throughout your premises. Does signal strength hold up enough to maintain connections as someone walks throughout the areas where you will place access point units?

> **Tip**
>
> Most Wi-Fi units come with utility software that can show you signal strength, packet transmission, and noise (interference) results as you move around. How to use this software, and where best to place access points, are topics discussed in Chapters 2 and 6. You might also want to try attaching indoor antennas to see how much they can boost the range of your transmissions.

CH
3

Test both range (how far) and throughput (how much). Test range by moving the portable further away from the access point. Test throughput by sending typical files back and forth between your access point and your portable. Time the transmissions and note how much data you successfully exchanged. Try to use files like those that will be actually exchanged by your employees in a typical day at work.

When you've found the best location for an access point, mark that position on the wall and describe the position on your blueprint. As a general rule, position access points in the center of smaller rooms if possible, to cover the entire room (rather than putting it on a wall). Also, usually the higher you locate the access point the greater its coverage area. Don't hide access points behind cubicle walls, bookcases, or near metal objects, such as filing cabinets.

5. Step 4 will have revealed areas, such as libraries with their signal-absorbing books, or high-humidity solaria, which will require additional access points and/or antennas, to provide full coverage. Mark your blueprints showing the best locations for these additional access points.

6. Attempt to identify possible sources of interference (microwave ovens, some portable phones, Bluetooth devices, some elevators and burglar alarms are the most likely culprits). Test these RF (radio frequency) sources by turning on the oven, using the phones, and so on. Watch your utility software's noise reports to see what effect the interference is having. Plan to add additional access points in noisy locations, or move the source of the problem. Sometimes a microwave oven can conveniently be repositioned, for example, within a break room so it causes no more problems.

If you want your Wi-Fi network to offer Internet connections, there are several ways to provide this connection. For instance, you can connect an access point directly to an

Internet connection (see Chapter 5, "The Internet Connection"). If you use this direct connection technique, ensure that any computers using this connection have firewall software installed.

Other setups employ Internet connection methods like network address translation (NAT). This arrangement usually includes firewall protection within the network itself, so client computers need not worry about invasion from Internet-based hackers. Estimate the impact of the type of Internet connections and number of access points you have on the throughput you need. How will you service the traffic that you expect? You can always add more access points and switch ISPs, but getting it right the first time can save both time and money. As you will see in Chapter 7, "Lighting Up the Neighborhood," for example, a campuswide Wi-Fi-based Internet connection could be seriously bogged down by enthusiastic file "sharing" activity.

8. If feasible, conduct a pilot test by installing a small, single-access-point Wi-Fi network involving a few of your average employees. This real-world survey can reveal throughput, roaming, range, or interference issues that a simpler site survey did not expose.

9. Take another look at your blueprint or layout diagram. It should now contain marks illustrating the location of access points, dead zones, roaming patterns, sources of interference, and all the users. See whether you can perhaps rearrange your office to reduce signal blockage. For example, are bookcases located all over the place inside the office? Moving the bookcases against the exterior walls might increase the range of your access points' coverage as much as 40–60%.

SETTING UP THE LAN

After you've finished your planning and purchased the equipment, you're ready to begin the installation. Here are the steps to take:

1. Physically install the Wi-Fi PCM cards into the portable computers, and the USB or PCI Wi-Fi units in desktop computers that will participate in your Wi-Fi LAN. In some cases the physical installation process triggers Windows plug-and-play feature. You can either install drivers and support software at this point, or use Control Panel's Add New Hardware utility in Step 8. For step-by-step explanations on how to install drivers and Wi-Fi utility software, see Chapter 2.

 Before installing drivers, firmware updates, or support software for Wi-Fi hardware, go to the manufacturer's Web site and download all the latest software for your Wi-Fi equipment. In our many hours of testing with various manufacturers' Wi-Fi equipment, we've found one nearly universal rule: Your installation will go much more smoothly if you download the support software from their Web site rather than relying on the software on the CD that ships with the equipment.

2. If you are adding Wi-Fi to an existing wire network, attach the necessary cables between the existing network's ethernet repeaters or switches and the Wi-Fi access point units.

3. Position the access point units, most of which include mounting hardware or other ways to secure them to walls or cabinets.

4. Position and attach any external antennas.

5. If a WAN is involved, make the necessary connections to it.

6. Set up your network operating system.

7. Install the drivers and utility software that came with the Wi-Fi equipment on the portables, desktop clients, and servers.

8. Using the utility software that came with the Wi-Fi equipment, set the parameters for the access points and the PCM cards or USB cards. These parameters are the SSID (network ID), any encryption settings, the Wi-Fi channel, and any settings unique to your hardware (such as network type). For step-by-step explanations on how to configure these settings, see Chapter 2. Some access points can be configured via utility software located in a Wi-Fi-equipped portable computer; other access points require physical serial port or other kinds of connections for their configuration. Other access points accept configuration via their ethernet connection.

THE TESTING PROCESS

CH
3

After you have the hardware and software installed, it's time to test your Wi-Fi LAN and iron out any kinks. This process begins by attempting to communicate between Wi-Fi-equipped computers. Precisely how you test depends on how your network is set up. Computers that should be able to share files with each other should be tested by attempting to access those files. Similarly, if printer sharing is enabled, test that from the various computers that are supposed to have printer access.

NO CONNECTION

If no connection at all can be established between a computer and an access point, check the following:

- Is encryption set the same way on both the computer and the access point? (Either off, or if on, using the same password and encryption system.)

- Is all the hardware correctly seated (Is the antenna, if any, correctly attached to the access point? Is the PCM card firmly seated in the computer? Is any USB connection firmly attached? Reattach and reseat these items to ensure connection.

- Do both the access point and the communicating computers share the same channel and SSID? It is possible to permit the access point to force nearby communicating Wi-Fi-equipped computers to adopt its channel number and SSID. If this is your intent (it permits roaming from access point to access point throughout a building), ensure that the computers are set to passively adopt the channel number and SSID of whatever access point is broadcasting in their area.

- Most printers, Wi-Fi hardware, and other hardware have either built-in self-test firmware, or utility software that can verify that they are operational. Run these tests to isolate any problem hardware if possible, before attempting to integrate that hardware into a network.

■ It's unlikely, but possible, that there is a hardware failure. If all the previous tests are passed but communication still doesn't work, try the following test. Can several portables communicate with this access point just fine, but one portable fails? Try swapping the PCM Wi-Fi card with a known-working card from one of the successful portables. If the bad computer now communicates, something was wrong with its previous PCM card. Similarly, if all the portables are working well with other access points, but fail with a particular access point—there's something wrong with that particular access point.

■ Far more likely than a hardware problem is a *cable* or *connection* problem. Wi-Fi is a radio broadcasting medium and it is, essentially, *wireless* of course. But it nonetheless requires wires to attach to cable modems, DSL units, and wire network repeaters and switches. Facing a communication problem, see whether you can isolate the problem to a particular area, then double-check wall plates, cables, and connections. Employ a cable tester if necessary. But we're getting away from Wi-Fi here, and into the realm of traditional wired networking tests. That's a topic beyond the scope of this book.

BAD CONNECTION

If the connection works, there can still be issues you must address. Here are some additional items to check:

■ Try sending and receiving files. If you notice that a request for a file on a remote machine keeps repeatedly trying to access that file, but continues to fail, check to see whether there is a source of interference such as a microwave oven, or whether network traffic has saturated the network's pipelines.

■ If things work fine when a few users are working, but slow down or stop when more users begin working, you are likely overloading your access point. You can try placing an additional access point right next to the existing one, tuned to a different channel, to see whether that unblocks the logjam. Or check to ensure that nearby access points are all using *different* channels (see "Channel Selection" later in this chapter). Finally, try repositioning the access point to see whether you can get it to a higher, or less obstructed, position.

■ Walk around the premises (*roam*, as it's called) to see whether a portable can connect to the various access points (cells) around the building.

■ See whether you can run applications on servers or peer machines from portables. See whether desktops can access files or run applications they are supposed to be able to access and run. (Note that some applications cannot be run over network connections—they require individual installation on each computer.)

CHANNEL DESIGN

You usually place access points so they do not significantly overlap each other's coverage area, then tune them to different channels (Wi-Fi offers channels from 1 to 11). *However, it matters which channels you choose!* Channels further apart numerically are further apart in frequency allocation (1 is closer to 3 than it is to 7). In a multi-access point installation, you don't want channel selection to cause the access points to interfere with each other.

Typically, you will choose channels 1, 6, and 11, to minimize problems. You will then use these channels in a way that maximizes the distance between repetitions of the same channel. For instance, in a long, narrow room, you would place them: 1, 6, 11, 1, 6, 11, 1, 6, 11, and so on. In a large square room, use this:

11		6	1
1		11	6
6		1	11
11		6	1

Wi-Fi transmissions go through floors as well as walls, so if you are setting up a Wi-Fi LAN in a multistory building, you will want to stagger the channels vertically as well as horizontally. (Revisualize the preceding pattern and think of it as representing the channels you would use for a four-story building.)

GOING BEYOND A SINGLE BUILDING

After you've shaken down your new Wi-Fi LAN in your main office building, perhaps you're feeling frisky and decide to go for the whole enchilada: all the buildings in your corporation.

Wi-Fi makes the job of connecting multiple locations somewhat easier. If you want to create a MAN, a metropolitan area network, you can use Wi-Fi radio itself, wireless microwave, or laser transmission methods.

THE ZAPPED GOOSE

There are problems, though, with outdoor laser communication. Two years ago I was on a conference call with several people at a publishing house when the line went dead. After the connection was reestablished about five minutes later, the publisher said, "It was a goose. I saw it fly between our buildings. We have a laser link on this phone and all it takes is one low-flying goose to break the connection." The goose wasn't hurt, though it's strange and rare to find a goose flying solo.

Weather, too, can play havoc with the transmission, and line-of-sight is essential. You must place the transmitter high enough that people can't look at the laser beam (hurting their eyes) or block the transmission.

Contact vendors AirFiber Inc. (`www.airfiber.com/index.htm`) or Terabeam Corp. (`www.terabeam.com/hom.html`) to see what's available and what kinds of solutions they can offer to common transmission problems for laser interbuilding communications.

CH
3

TRADITIONAL WI-FI

It's also possible to simply post antennas, connected to Wi-Fi access points, high up outside a pair of buildings. Here, too, a site survey is wise, to test the range and throughput capacity, but also to best determine how to orient your antenna. Directional outdoor antennas, in particular, require careful calibration to get the most signal throughput for your dollar.

With Wi-Fi antennas, line-of-sight is, of course, essential, and you must also take into consideration possible natural sources of interference such as fog, rain, general humidity, and so on. Man-made radio interference, as well as multipath distortion, are considerations, too.

If you are working with a bright, reflective environment, you'll likely have to cope with multipath distortion (see Chapter 6, "Putting an Antenna on Your Roof and Elsewhere"). If so, look into a technique called *antenna diversity*, which can help with this particular problem. You employ two antennas simultaneously and combine uncorrelated signals using special electronics.

Tip

Antennas almost always do better when placed higher—either outdoors or indoors. This is particularly important outdoors because you don't want traffic, pedestrians, or geese blocking the signal. Normally, though, there won't be sources of electricity available for mounting an access point near an outside antenna. Follow the building codes and your landlord's requirements, of course, but note that some equipment can be powered through the ethernet cable that connects to your access point. This could help you avoid the cost of running additional electric wire.

4

AT HOME AND AT WORK

In this chapter

This chapter takes you on a tour of several real-world Wi-Fi installations. Here are five case studies, stories illustrating how real people have benefited from Wi-Fi at home or in public places. You'll doubtless discover uses for Wi-Fi in this chapter that you never imagined.

CASE STUDY: THE AUTHOR AT HOME

Wi-Fi has certainly made a difference in my house (this is co-author Richard Mansfield speaking). I've found that it's a great way to synergize your home computing. Dependable, inexpensive, and efficient, Wi-Fi allows you the freedom to use your computers in ways you hadn't previously thought of.

Like many people, I have more than one computer in my house. In fact, because I write computer books, I have two desktops and a portable. The two desktops are a result of having to buy a new computer every couple of years—just so I'll have the latest equipment so I can write about memory-hungry beta software.

When I began writing this book, the first Wi-Fi loaner equipment started arriving from vendors. I expected that Wi-Fi would offer some new conveniences, but little did I realize how much a wireless network would change things around my house. I have to send all those loaned Wi-Fi units back in a few weeks, but I'm going to go out and buy my own Wi-Fi hardware. I simply don't want to be without it. I don't want to go back to my old ways.

NO MORE PAPER ON THE WALLS

How has Wi-Fi changed things? Let me count the ways. First a small example. I'm fond of cooking and I keep all my recipes on my desktop computer in my study. Once a week or so I get excited and decide to whip up something special. I look up the recipe, print a copy of it, and then walk into the kitchen and hang the paper on the kitchen wall so I can follow the instructions. No more. Yesterday I didn't bother with the printer or the paper. I just took my portable into the kitchen and flipped it open on the butcher block island. It was easy to read the recipe off the screen. Multiply this little convenience by a couple dozen other new efficiencies, and you begin to see how handy Wi-Fi is.

The key idea here is *portable*. With Wi-Fi, my computer can go where I go. No longer do I have to go into my study when I want to look up information, do e-mail, print something, or surf the Internet. For example, my study has a nice view, but my favorite view is from the dining room with its floor-to-ceiling picture windows. Now, if I want a change, I open the portable on the dining room table and do a little research for a half hour or so. When finished, I send the file via Wi-Fi to my desktop computer. Then, I go back to the study and the file is sitting there waiting for me.

FOREIGN VISITORS

The first really major change I noticed from my new Wi-Fi capability was how much guests appreciated the broadcast Internet connection. Until you travel a few days to a place where you can't connect to the Internet, you don't fully realize how dependent you've grown on getting online for news, mail, and all the rest.

One friend, an Athenian, spends a few weeks at our house twice a year. He's a writer, too, and he goes nowhere without his portable. During previous visits, we stepped on each other's toes trying to share my one cable modem Internet connection.

He had to take the time to set up his own account in my copy of Outlook Express. He had to politely wait until I was through using my desktop machine before he could even check his mail or read the news and the "football" scores from Greece.

And little things that you normally don't notice can became annoying. For example, the auto-completion feature in Windows gets mixed up when two people share the same computer. I'm used to typing *Ri* and *Richard Mansfield* automatically appears in a list—so I don't have to type my whole name. But when my friend uses my computer for a few days, *his* auto-completion terms get mixed in with mine. His logon names start showing up in my password screens, and so on. My private correspondence, the caches of all my recent Internet surfing, his personal e-mail, his business transactions—all these sometimes private communications become public to the person you share your machine with.

He sometimes left the Cyrillic alphabet selected, so I would sit down and everything on screen was Greek to me. He set up some new folders for himself on my C:\ drive, and his Web surfing caused changes to my Internet Explorer History list. Worst of all, I'd find lots of *hair* in the keyboard because he twists his beard when thinking, and he's always thinking. All these little aggravations accumulate and put a strain on your friendship.

One solution to computer-sharing is to set up separate identities. But then you have to switch identities every time you want to simply check your e-mail. And it doesn't solve problems like the twisted whiskers issue.

CH
4

What a difference Wi-Fi made. Like me, Evangelos likes working on our dining room table. He enjoys looking out on the lawn that goes down to the river. It's especially nice when, in the early morning, the mists rise off the slow moving waters. He visited a few weeks ago, and we stuck a Wi-Fi PCM card into his portable. Now he could do his writing, surfing, and e-mailing right from his own computer, without having to bother at all with my desktop machine. He could freely move between the guest room and the dining room, as the mood struck. Soon he was as happy as a Greek clam.

No Legacy Connections

Wi-Fi also solved another problem during my friend's visit.

In the past, when he wanted to send chapters with large screenshot graphics files to his publisher, we had difficulties getting them from his laptop onto the Internet. The files would not fit onto a 1.4M diskette, so we couldn't transfer them to my desktop machine that way. We had to either create a direct (serial port) connection, or wire his laptop to my telephone line so he could (very slowly) modem the files.

Evangelos bought one of the latest laptops. The vendor boasts that it has no "legacy" connections. This means that it doesn't have a serial port! Fortunately, thanks to Wi-Fi, his laptop is always able to use my cable modem Internet connection. That saves time and money every time he finishes a chapter.

I could go on. Wi-Fi makes multicomputer game playing a snap. All the computers can use my printers—no more copying files to disks, then transferring those files into the main, printer-connected machine. And there are those afternoons when it's just more pleasant to take the laptop down by the pool and do the writing under the rustling oak trees by the river.

But enough about me. Let's expand our coverage of real-world Wi-Fi installations. Next up: one way they use Wi-Fi in Vegas.

CASE STUDY: CHECKING IN AT THE VENETIAN HOTEL

If you are a "road warrior"—or are not a road warrior, but have simply been part of a large group checking into a hotel—you will appreciate The Venetian Resort-Hotel-Casino's 802.11b wireless quick check-in application.

The Venetian, opened in 1999 and located in Las Vegas, Nevada, is a premier, upscale mega-resort. According to The Venetian's Internet Marketing Manager Chris Stacey, "The Venetian is in the forefront of technology innovations in the hotel industry. We like to pilot progressive new technologies in the light of how they will convenience guests. Other organizations in the hospitality industry will take a look at what we're doing, and sometimes decide to emulate it."

The goal of the check-in application is to eliminate check-in lines at the 3,036 suite resort. Clerks meet arriving guests at any of the hotel entrances. The clerk uses a Symbol Technologies model SPT 1740 handheld computer running the Palm operating system to take a swipe of the guest's credit card. (The Symbol handheld is strapped to the clerk's wrist.)

The resort's wireless LAN, an 802.11b network, is used to verify the credit card information and determine which room has been assigned to the guest. Next, the clerk uses a room-key encoder device, worn at the clerk's waist, and connected to the Symbol handheld, to generate a room key for the guest.

Mr. Stacey notes that the application is very flexible. "We don't always use it," he says. "It depends on what is needed. Sometimes fixed check-in registration works fine. At other times, for example, when we have certain conventions in-house, the wireless check-in application can be deployed to prevent bottlenecks. Compared with other wireless technologies, 802.11b is like an SUV. It may not be a sports car, but it is very versatile: You can drive it in the city, or off-road, and the price is very economical. We are so pleased with the technology that we are currently looking at other ways we can deploy it to improve our guest experience."

In the backend, the wireless check-in application connects to Cisco wireless hardware and the IBM AS/400 system that runs the hotel reservations systems. Stacey notes that it is critical that the reservations system is real-time, rather than batched, so that the wireless check-in system can accurately give out rooms. Because the hotel sometimes turns over thousands of rooms in a single day, a batched system could not guarantee that rooms given away were truly open.

The Lansa development environment was used to custom-build The Venetian's reservation system and the 802.11b quick check-in application. Stacey notes that the entire cost for the wireless project, including custom software and hardware, was under $100,000.

CASE STUDY: ONLINE AT AN AIRPORT

Wayport, Inc. is a privately held company based in Austin, Texas, in the business of supplying high-speed wireless networking services to customers of hotels and airports. Another important wireless ISP (or WISP) that offers Wi-Fi services in some airports is MobileStar, described in "Case Study: Online at Starbucks."

Generally, Wayport sells access on a pay-as-you-go basis. You can also sign up with Wayport for a bulk purchase of access time at a discount.

Wayport operates on a *concessionaire* model—meaning that airports get a portion of the revenue generated by Wayport in their facilities.

Currently, Wayport provides wireless access to all terminals and gate areas in four airports: Austin-Bergstrom, Dallas/Fort Worth, Seattle-Tacoma, and San Jose. For example, in the San Jose airport, Wayport provides six Access Points in Terminal A, and six Access Points in Terminal C, pretty much blanketing the airport.

Generally, all you need to get Internet access through Wayport in one of these airports is a portable computer equipped with a Wi-Fi (802.11b) card (and your credit card). The process is very simple. With a 802.11b card in place, boot your laptop. Next, open a Web browser. The Wayport connection screen should appear, which guides you through the process of registering with Wayport (see Figure 4.1). There is generally no reason to change any of your network settings to work with the Wayport service (but see the related Tips).

CH

4

Figure 4.1
To log on at an airport served by Wayport, such as San Jose International, just open your browser (you may have to set your network name (SSID) to "Wayport_Access").

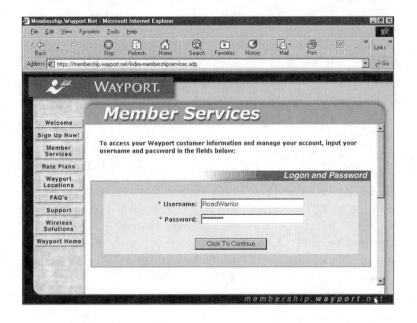

Setting the SSID

In some cases in order to get the Wayport wireless service to work, you will need to change the setting for the Service Set Identifier (SSID), also known as the "network name." If you don't see the Wayport welcome screen when you open your browser, you should change your SSID to "Wayport_Access" (note that the underscore is required, and the SSID *is* case sensitive).

Generally, the SSID can be entered using the configuration tool for your Wi-Fi card (or in the Properties dialog box for the card in the My Network Properties dialog box). See your product documentation for more information.

Tip

In some cases, the security policies in place at your company may require you to change your SMTP server to `mail.wayport.net` before you will be able to send e-mail.

How much does the Wayport service cost? We're so glad you asked…

Currently, Wayport charges on a per-connection basis. You should know that a connection is defined as unlimited use of the service in a single location for a single day, in particular, until midnight of the same day in airports. You can log off and on as often as you'd like. (The Wayport connection definition is different in hotels, where the "turn into a pumpkin" hour is defined by checkout time rather than midnight.)

Connections purchased on an ad-hoc basis in airports cost $6.95 each. If you prepay in advance, as a Wayport member you can buy a block of ten connections for $49.50 (so the unit cost is $4.95). You probably won't be surprised to learn that corporations can also negotiate group rates.

In general, users are enthusiastic about the service on the philosophy that if you have to be stuck in an airport you may as well surf, and if you are surfing it's great for it to be fast and wireless. More than 70% of business travelers already carry laptops, and as Wi-Fi becomes increasingly popular, more and more of these users will turn to services provided by Wayport and other services providers to spend their time in airports more productively.

CASE STUDY: CONNECTING AT STARBUCKS

Starbucks, the chain of coffee houses, was seeing more and more people come into its shops to do business. These ranged from business people to college students, all of whom wanted to sip café au lait or latte while they worked. Starting in mid-2001, Starbucks made the decision to facilitate these customers by setting up network accessibility for them in all its stores. On the other hand, Starbucks couldn't have a lot of wires trailing all over the place (or someone might trip on them and spill that latte). The natural answer was wireless Wi-Fi 802.11b networking.

WHAT IS MOBILESTAR?

MobileStar is one of the largest wireless Internet Service Providers, sometimes known by the acronym WISP. Founded in December 1996, MobileStar Network Corporation hosts a wireless, broadband communications network that allows subscribers to access the Internet and their corporate intranet remotely from public locations including more than 1,400 hotels, airports, restaurants, conference centers, and coffeehouses. Currently, Mobilestar offers its services in about 700 locations, of which approximately 500 are Starbucks Coffee shops. According to Ali Tabassi, the Chief Technology Officer of MobileStar, by the end of 2003 about 75% of the Starbucks shops—or 4,000 locations—will have MobileStar's wireless Wi-Fi access.

MobileStar's service is subscriber-based intended for what Mr. Tabassi describes as "public hot spots." Mr. Tabassi states, "Historically, wireless access was done with proprietary client software that assigns an IP to the laptop. When 802.11b and Wi-Fi came along, it was a golden opportunity for us to go to open standards. We have at least T1 connectivity to each location we serve, with Access Points and sometimes routers and switches connected via the backend broadband connection to an access control node located in a central network aggregation point."

Mr. Tabassi says that he has often been asked the question of what happens when there are two Wi-Fi providers in the same location. "If you have set your network name, or SSID, to one provider, in our case MobileStar with a capital M and S, you will, of course, be connected to that provider. If you don't set the network name, you will be connected to whichever provider has a stronger signal at your exact location."

According to Mr. Tabassi, MobileStar's ability to do real-time billing for usage gives it the capability of being a "roaming" provider for wireline ISP, or wireless providers who serve a different geographic footprint. So you might want to check to see whether a service provider you already have an account with allows you to use the MobileStar network.

Mr. Tabassi says that as a public provider, which necessarily implies using unencrypted transmissions, security sometimes causes concern. He believes that, as in any connection to the Internet, all users should install a personal firewall to protect their data. He suggests that corporate users should employ a VPN (Virtual Private Network) program to get point-to-point access to corporate data and protect it from unauthorized access (see Chapter 8, "Security and Encryption," for more information on firewalls and VPNs).

MOBILESTAR AND STARBUCKS

MobileStar has been selected by Starbucks to supply wireless Internet access in all its locations (currently about 4,000 stores across the country). When the rollout is complete in 2004, MobileStar projects that Starbucks will account for more than 75% of its locations.

MobileStar brings a wire-line T1 connection into each Starbucks. Customers connect to the T1 line via a wireless Access Point using hardware supplied by Cisco and Compaq and software developed using Microsoft tools.

CH

4

FINDING AN "UNWIRED" STARBUCKS NEAR YOU

Currently, most of the Starbucks equipped with Wi-Fi 802.11b wireless networking are located in or near San Jose, San Francisco, and Seattle.

The easiest way to find out whether the Starbucks you will be near has Wi-Fi is to use the mapping tool on the MobileStar Web site.

First, go to www.mobilestar.com (see Figure 4.2).

Figure 4.2
The MobileStar Web site provides the easiest way to find locations of "unwired" Starbucks coffee shops.

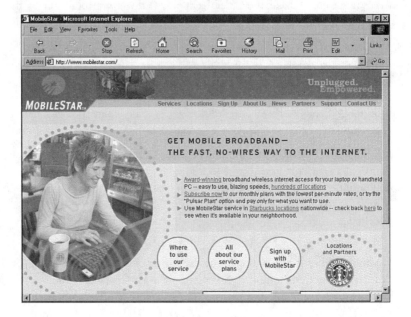

Click the Starbucks Locations link. A page providing information about the Starbucks wireless networking services will open as shown in Figure 4.3.

Next, click View Location Map. A map showing MobileStar North American locations will open (see Figure 4.4). You can filter the map to only display Starbucks Coffee locations using the drop-down box in the upper-right corner.

Figure 4.3
The MobileStar Web
site has Starbucks
status updates.

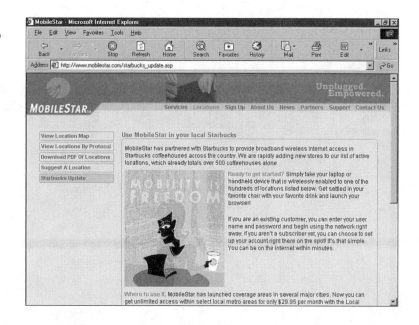

Figure 4.4
You can use the
dynamic map to
locate an "unwired"
Starbucks.

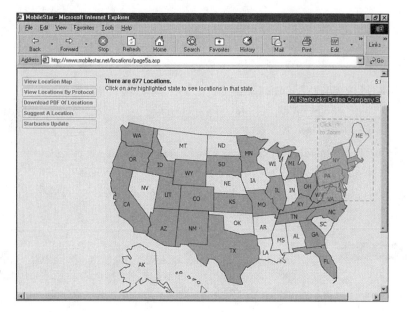

CH

4

Click on the general area you are interested in; for example, the state of California. The Starbucks stores with Wi-Fi networking in the area you selected will be displayed (see Figure 4.5).

Figure 4.5
Starbucks shops with Wi-Fi networking available in your area are displayed.

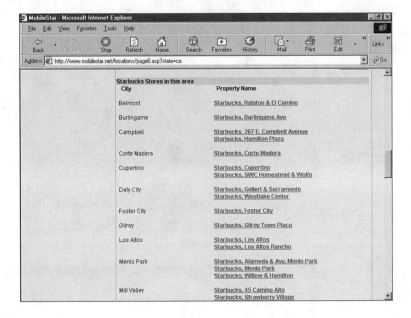

SIGNING UP WITH MOBILESTAR

It's easy to sign up with MobileStar in advance (or you can sign up in "real time" when you visit a Starbucks).

To sign up in advance, go to the MobileStar Web site, `www.mobilestar.com`. Choose the Sign Up link from the toolbar. The initial sign-up screen will open (see Figure 4.6).

This initial screen gives you the chance to log on via a corporate account. You can also enter any promotional codes you may have.

Tip

Some Starbucks locations will have MobileStar brochures with a promotional discount code you can use to sign up at a reduced rate. Check the front counter when you order your beverage of choice.

Figure 4.6
It's easy to sign up for a prepayment plan in advance on the MobileStar Web site.

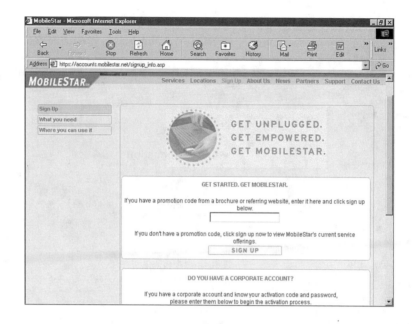

Next, select Sign Up. You will select a payment plan, as shown in Figure 4.7.

Figure 4.7
MobileStar offers a number of different payment plans.

CH
4

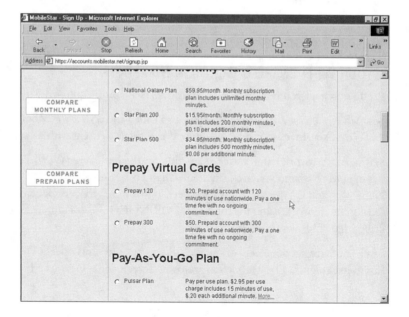

Currently, the most popular plans are the prepaid 120 minutes (the cost is $20.00) and the pay-as-you-go plan ($.20 per minute, with a $3.00 minimum per usage).

After you have selected a plan, you'll see a standard credit card billing screen (see Figure 4.8). The screen is also used to select your MobileStar Login name and password.

Figure 4.8
To sign up, you need to give MobileStar a credit card and pick a login name and password.

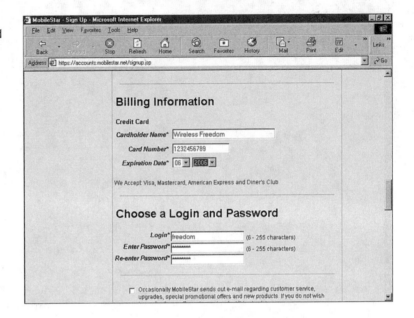

Click Sign Up Now, and you're ready to go.

USING YOUR WI-FI ENABLED LAPTOP IN STARBUCKS

Pretty much all you need to surf at Starbucks is a laptop equipped with a Wi-Fi PC card.

You will need to set the network name, also called the SSID, to "MobileStar." Note that this is case sensitive, so it must be entered exactly as written, with a capital M and S.

Setting the network name varies depending on the hardware (Wi-Fi PC card) you have and the operating system you are using. See Chapter 2, "Setting Up Your Personal Wireless Network," and Chapter 6, "The Internet Connection," for more details. Figure 4.9 shows setting the network name for the Lucent ORiNOCO Silver card, using the administrative utility that ships with the card.

After you have set your network name, all you have to do is open a Web browser such as Internet Explorer. The MobileStar welcome screen will appear (see Figure 4.10).

Figure 4.9
To connect to the MobileStar network, the Network Name must be set to "MobileStar."

Figure 4.10
The MobileStar screen automatically appears when you open your browser in Starbucks.

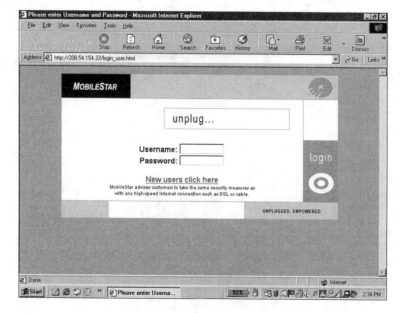

Сн
4

If you have already signed up with MobileStar, just enter your ID and password (see Figure 4.11). Otherwise, you can start the sign up process by selecting New Users click here to give your credit card and obtain a username and password.

Figure 4.11
Enter your Username
and Password to log on.

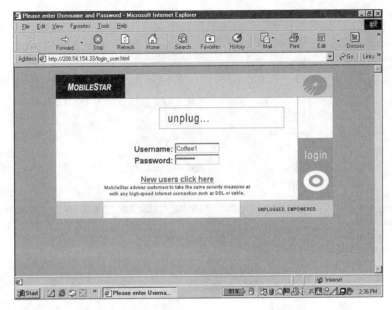

That's all there is to it! Enjoy your "surf and latte" (see Figure 4.12).

Figure 4.12
You can enjoy coffee
and surfing the
Internet at a Wi-Fi
equipped "wireless"
Starbucks.

CASE STUDY: A SMALL OFFICE ENVIRONMENT

Oppedahl & Larson LLP is a law firm offering patent, copyright, trademark, trade secret, and other intellectual property services. This is a small firm, located in scenic Dillon, Colorado. Carl Oppedahl and Marina Larson, two distinguished former New York intellectual property attorneys, are the partners who founded it. The firm's mission is to "provide the highest quality legal services to clients while using up-to-date technological support to achieve high levels of efficiency and responsiveness to client needs."

Oppedahl & Larson uses 802.11b wireless networking in its offices, as well as in the two partner's homes, to supplement wire-line LANs. The public office and the two home offices are connected by a point-to-point microwave WAN. According to Mr. Oppedal, "when we investigated, we found that 802.11b access points and PC cards were a reliable and cost-effective way to provide mobility within our office and homes, augmenting our existing wired networks."

Mr. Oppedahl says that mobility is important. For example, he notes, "often I'll be working at my desk, and I'll realize I need information from somewhere else. With wireless connectivity, I can take my computer down the hall, type in what I need, and carry my computer back to my desk. Last week, I was leaving the office, and I was all the way to the parking lot when I heard the computer beep saying a new e-mail had come in. I was able to check it right then and there. It turned out to be very important, and if I didn't have the wireless networking, I wouldn't have gotten it until the next day."

He adds that "another advantage is that it gives us experience with the wireless cards so that when they travel to places that have wireless facilities, they'll have their computers configured, ready to go, and operable in those settings." Not only will the firm's employees be able to work in "on the go" environments such as airports and coffee shops such as Starbucks, but also, according to Mr. Oppedahl, "in the near future, all offices that you visit will offer 802.11b wireless access to guests."

Mr. Oppedahl states, "We are much more productive traveling. Wireless accessibility will enable me to do work that I wouldn't have been able to do otherwise. I now only pick hotels that have high-speed Internet access. It is still usually only provided in the guest room. But I take an access point, such as the Agere ORiNOCO Residential Gateway (RG-1000) with me, plug it into the jack, and others in my party can use my Internet connection as long as they are within range. This provides an easy way for people traveling together to conveniently share files and share one connection to the Internet."

Each of the attorney's homes has a wired network. Before they began using wireless products, the attorneys were limited to where they could work in their homes. They were confined to locations that had ethernet jacks that connected to the LAN. The Wi-Fi cards now enable the lawyers to move around their homes and work anywhere, regardless of where jacks are located. The attorneys will often work in their kitchens while drinking their morning coffee, and an hour later be working on the same notebook computer at their desk in their office.

CH

4

Mr. Oppedahl states, "There may be some reasons that offices might prefer wire-line networks. These include security, and the knowledge that a neighbor with an 802.11b network, or other device that operates in the 2.4 Gigaherz spectrum, won't interfere so that the network will behave the same tomorrow as it does today. That said, 802.11b wireless networking has given us a great deal of flexibility, and has enhanced our efficiency and productivity."

CHAPTER **5**

THE INTERNET CONNECTION

In this chapter

Our research for this book has taught us one lesson above all others when installing Wi-Fi equipment. It is often essential that you first download the latest driver/utility software package from the manufacturer of your Wi-Fi equipment. Don't depend on the CD that ships with your Wi-Fi hardware. With surprising regularity, we have found that attempting to use the CD bundled with your Wi-Fi hardware merely wastes time. If possible, get on the Internet and download the latest software before beginning the installation process. Note, too, that there is often firmware (a reprogrammable chip) in Wi-Fi access points and residential gateway units. This also can require upgrading. There will likely be an .EXE file in the support software you download which, when run, will automatically seek out and upgrade your Wi-Fi unit.

The Internet is fast becoming as important as your computer's hard drive. Not that long ago, you spent 95% of your computer time interacting with applications and data stored right there in your machine. Perhaps an hour or two a week was spent connected via modem to bulletin board services and such.

Now many users have cable modem or DSL (high-speed phone) Internet connections that are always on. No phone call is needed. Also, people are spending a continually increasing amount of their computing time online: The Internet is proving to be an unparalleled research tool, as well as a terrific source of current news and entertainment.

Experts predict that soon we'll move some or all the actual contents of our hard drives onto the Internet. You might subscribe to applications like Quicken, rather than buy a CD and install it on your hard drive. Perhaps each time you use Quicken online, you will be charged a small fee, or maybe there will be a monthly subscription cost. Also, your data files, like your Quicken information, could also be stored on a server somewhere online. The great advantage of moving entirely off your hard drive is that you can then use your applications and your data anywhere—you're not tied to a particular computer located in a particular room. You can just as easily file your Quicken-computed tax forms while riding a train as while sitting in front of your desktop computer.

BROADCAST YOUR BROADBAND CONNECTION

Not coincidentally, cable modem and DSL connections are broadband (fast). After you get a broadband connection, ordinary 56K phone line connections seem excruciatingly slow. With a broadband connection, you don't think twice about downloading an 8 Meg software update; with an ordinary 56K connection, you would have to tie up your telephone for hours to get that much information into your hard drive.

Cable modem or DSL connections—let's refer to them collectively as *broadband connections*— quickly become essential to anyone who is lucky enough to have one. Estimates are that 12% of home users currently enjoy broadband Internet, and broadband is rapidly penetrating both the home and business markets.

However, you don't want to have to install separate connections for each computer on your Wi-Fi LAN. Separate installation and wiring would be quite expensive, and, after all, wireless networking is, by definition, all about avoiding wiring whenever possible. Also, the monthly charge for a cable modem or DSL connection averages $550 per year. The solution? Broadcast your always-on, high-speed broadband connection over your Wi-Fi network.

Note that putting your Internet connection onto your Wi-Fi cell does not mean that each user must watch the same Internet page. If dad surfs to CNN, junior can surf to the Lakers basketball page—they both have the ability to surf wherever they want, just as all the TVs connected to cable in your house do not have to be tuned to the same channel.

Adding Wi-Fi connections to a single access point does, of course, slow down the throughput. If you have, say, five Wi-Fi connections to a single broadband Internet connection (via cable/modem or via DSL) you will decrease Internet speed. However, unless several people are simultaneously downloading or uploading files, it's likely you won't notice much degradation in speed. A single access point Wi-Fi can support up to around 18 connections.

The actual number of permitted connections depends on the manufacturer: Agere permits 18, Sony 16, but each of them begins by assigning 10.0.1.1 as the access point's Internet Protocol (IP) address, then on up to through 10.0.1.17, or .19, as the case may be. This IP address assignment is automatically handled by the access point—it ensures that each USB or PCM client unit gets its own, individual IP address.

There's nothing magical about the number 16 or 18, and a variety of ways, to set up networks to have more nodes. You can also connect the access point to a traditional network router, which also connects to wire-line clients. If you want, you could connect multiple access points to the router up to the router's capacity. However at some point, a simple single Wi-Fi cable or DSL connection for all these clients will become unusable just because there are too many people at the same drinking fountain, so to speak, and the throughput would bog down too much.

A Wi-Fi access point includes, among other electronics, a transceiving antenna: It provides a connection to the Wi-Fi LAN for several computers equipped with only a Wi-Fi PCM card or USB unit. You can also think of an access point as comparable to a traditional wired network router, and the Wi-Fi PCM cards as NICs (Network Interface Cards).

Access points (AP) also include an ethernet uplink to connect the Wi-Fi units to a wired network, and 802.11b bridging software. As you saw in Chapter 3, "Larger Scale Wi-Fi Setups," you extend the coverage area of a Wi-Fi LAN by deploying APs throughout your office, hotel, campus, or whatever physical plant you want to "light up" (*lighting up* is the colorful phrase that refers to creating a coverage area where Wi-Fi transmissions are available).

But back to this chapter's main topic: broadcasting your broadband. There's something very cool about having high-speed Internet available to all the computers in your house, and to the portable computers of friends who come stay in the guest room. In fact, some of our friends have said, "If you don't provide wireless 802.11b access for us when we come to visit, you're just not with it."

Let's see how to boost a cable modem (or DSL) connection from its traditional service for one computer, to a housewide or small officewide connection using Wi-Fi.

CH

5

> **Tip**
>
> A DSL to 802.11b connection works exactly the same way as a cable modem connection. So the instructions you'll find in this chapter that refer to cable modem can be applied as well to a DSL installation.

INSTALLING A WI-FI CABLE MODEM CONNECTION

Each manufacturer's setup process differs somewhat, but the basic steps are the same: Install the hardware, then the drivers (if necessary), install the manufacturer's custom utility programs, and use a utility program to contact and set up the access point unit.

In this example, we'll demonstrate how to use the Sony Vaio access point unit (PCWA-A200). Take a look at Figure 5.1.

Figure 5.1
A Wi-Fi access point can provide a broadband Internet connection to multiple Wi-Fi-equipped computers.

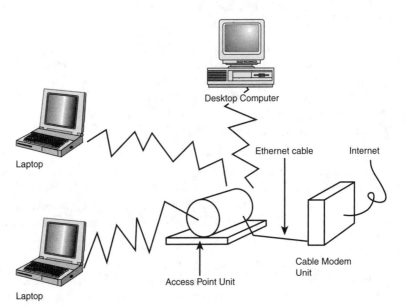

ATTACHING THE CABLE MODEM UNIT TO THE WI-FI ACCESS POINT UNIT

If you are installing a brand-new cable modem Internet connection at the same time you are installing the Wi-Fi access point, get your cable modem or DSL Internet connection working on one computer before continuing with the steps that follow in this chapter. Reason: You'll probably only get tech support from the cable or DSL company while connecting to a single machine. "We are not responsible for helping with networks." There are lots of things that can go wrong when establishing a broadband connection to the Internet, and you, dear reader, need to first get your Internet connection working before you attach Wi-Fi equipment.

So, assuming you have your Internet connection working, follow these steps:

1. Your first step when setting up a Wi-Fi cable modem connection is to turn off the power to your computer and the cable modem unit.

2. Then disconnect the ethernet cable that connects the cable modem unit to the ethernet card in your computer. Simply disconnect the computer end—leave the ethernet cable plugged into the cable modem unit.

3. Plug one end of the ethernet cable into the jack in the access point, and the other end into the jack in the cable modem unit.

   Use the same ethernet cable that is used to attach your desktop computer to the cable modem unit. (It's a flexible category 5 ethernet cable with a 10BASE-T connector.)

4. Now plug both the access point and the cable modem unit back into electric outlets.

INSTALLING DRIVERS

This step may or may not be necessary, depending on whether or not you currently have a Wi-Fi USB unit or Wi-Fi PCM card already installed on your computer. If not, plug in the unit or card now. That will alert Windows Plug and Play feature that new hardware has been added to your system. Follow the instructions in Chapter 2, "Setting Up Your Personal Wireless Network," to install the correct driver. If you already have a Wi-Fi device installed, you can skip this step. Note that every computer you want to communicate with your Wi-Fi access point requires an installed Wi-Fi card, or USB unit.

INSTALLING SUPPORT SOFTWARE

In addition to any drivers needed to run Wi-Fi units attached to your computer, Wi-Fi equipment also includes other utility software. There will likely be a utility that can test links, modify settings, and otherwise manage your Wi-Fi unit and connection. ORiNOCO calls this the Client Manager and Sony calls it the Wireless Palette.

This software comes on the CD with your Wi-Fi equipment, but as the warning at the beginning of this chapter suggests, try to download the latest software from the manufacturer's Web site. Then run the setup program to install this software on a computer that has a Wi-Fi PCM card or USB unit.

When you are using an access point unit as we are in this chapter, the access point is connected by cable to the cable modem, ordinary phone line, ISDN router, or DSL unit. But the access point unit is not connected physically to any of your computers. To configure the access point, you must run utility software that employs the USB or PCM card that is physically attached to your computer. That utility software communicates with access point via radio waves from your USB or PCM unit—to permit you to configure the access point. Here's how it works.

To configure the Sony Vaio access point, run the Custom Access Point Setup Utility (from Start, Programs, Wireless Lan). You should see a dialog box similar to the one shown in Figure 5.2.

CH

5

Figure 5.2
Use a utility like this to scan for your access point.

With your access point unit plugged in to the wall outlet (and also connected by ethernet cable to your cable modem unit), click the Scan button shown in Figure 5.2.

After the scanning detects your access point, a report is displayed as shown in Figure 5.3.

Figure 5.3
Use this dialog box to specify the type of connection, channel number, encryption, and SSID (network name).

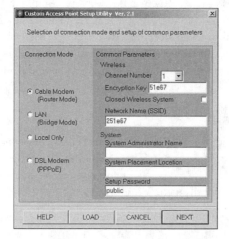

Sony access points automatically assign an SSID based on a 6-character ID that is also found on the bottom of the hardware unit. It also defaults to an encryption key which is the last five characters of the SSID. You can of course change these defaults. In this example, you can delete the encryption key. This way it will be simpler for PCM cards and USB units to make contact with your access point.

Leave the Cable Modem (router mode) selected unless you are setting up a DSL or LAN connection. You can also leave the channel number set to 1 unless that interferes with other Wi-Fi broadcast equipment in your home or office. Leave the SSID name alone, too. It doesn't matter in this setup because the SSID and channel will be broadcast to any PCM or USB units in the vicinity and they will automatically accept these defaults.

Note that the Sony Vaio unit we're installing here makes a distinction between a connection to cable modem versus DSL. Generally, though, there is no difference from the viewpoint of an access point between DSL and cable. With the Vaio, select DSL for DSL, but for many Wi-Fi access points, there is no configuration difference between cable and DSL.

Click the Next button. A message comes up warning you that your access point will be configured to No Encryption (because you erased the key). Unless you have a compelling reason to do otherwise, simply click the OK button to close this dialog box and leave the encryption turned off.

Click the Upload button. Your settings are transmitted to the firmware in the access point. Now you're ready to roll.

TESTING, TESTING, TESTING

You should now be able to run Internet Explorer and it should automatically connect to the Internet via your cable modem connection. If you see the famous message The page cannot be displayed, as shown in Figure 5.4, close Internet Explorer and we'll try a few things.

Figure 5.4
Uh-oh, something's amiss here. Let's fix the problem.

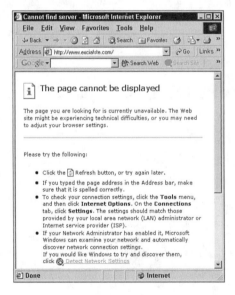

If this is the first time you've used this broadband connection with this computer, run the installation software that came with your cable modem unit. Recall my earlier point about getting your Internet connection working with one computer before introducing the Wi-Fi factor. Generally, you can fire up Internet Explorer and get onto the Internet without having to install any support software. However, it could be necessary (you may have to contact your ISP—Internet Service Provider).

To set up Outlook Express or some other e-mail application, you will have to run a setup routine that came with your cable modem, if only to define mail and news accounts that specify the correct username and password; e-mail address; and POP3, SMTP, and News server names. All this information, and how to set up an e-mail account in Windows, should be supplied by your cable modem ISP.

Note

Multiple users with separate e-mail will each need their own e-mail account. Some ISPs will provide more than one e-mail account, in some cases for a fee. @home, for example, will give you up to five. That's not enough for many users with families, or for SOHO businesses. If you have a hosted Web site, it's likely that your Web host will provide multiple e-mail accounts if you need them, usually for an additional fee. You can also purchase inexpensive standalone POP accounts from companies such as Domain Direct, http://www.domaindirect.com. (It costs $40 per year, includes a URL such as www.janedoe.com, so the SMTP and POP servers are mail.janedoe.com). Note that most hosting sites provide as many e-mail accounts as the subscriber wants, and many of the better sites provide a way for these e-mail accounts to be set up using a Web interface by the subscriber. Some do have limits on the individual, specific e-mail accounts (rather than using generic e-mail names that can be retrieved using the main account name), but we've found that the better sites don't offer fewer than ten. There are also free mail accounts (hotmail.com, iname.com, and a whole bunch more) that provide free e-mail (with some limitations such as archive size).

ADDING OTHER COMPUTERS TO THE CONNECTION

If you are using the access point setup described earlier, it is easy to connect additional computers to this same broadband Internet connection.

Tip

802.11b is a standard, and all 802.11b equipment labeled "Wi-Fi" is guaranteed compatible, so it doesn't matter if you use a Sony access point, but an associate visits your office and his Wi-Fi PCM card is an Agere ORiNOCO model. He should be able to wander into your access point's range, turn on his laptop, and his PCM card should start accepting information from your access point (channel, SSID, or network id name, and an IP address to use with your broadband Internet connection). These issues are described later in more detail, but don't worry whether you're mixing and matching brands of Wi-Fi equipment. They are supposed to work together.

First you must ensure that the IP address is automatically assigned to your connection. (If you are not using Windows 2000, see Chapter 2 for details on how to access a connection in NT or Windows 98/95.)

In Windows 2000's Windows Explorer, right-click My Network Places and choose Properties from the Context menu. The Network and Dialup Connections dialog box appears. Look under the Device Name column. You should see a description of the connection to your Wi-Fi USB or PCM unit. (If you don't see this connection, look at Chapter 2 for instructions on adding a Wi-Fi USB unit or PCM card to your computer.)

The Device Name displayed in the Network and Dialup Connections dialog box will be something like ORiNOCO USB Card or LinkSys Card or Sony Wireless PC Card or some such. Double-click this connection to open its Status dialog box. Then click the Properties button in the Status dialog box.

Scroll down in the Properties dialog box until you see the Internet Protocol (TCP/IP) component listed. Click it to select that component. Click Properties. You should now click the Obtain an IP Address Automatically option button, and also click the option button that says Obtain DNS Server Address Automatically. Click OK twice to close both dialog boxes, then click Close to shut the Local Area Connection Status dialog box.

At this point, you should be able to follow the instructions in Chapter 2 to use the utility software that came with your Wi-Fi hardware to test your link to the Wi-Fi access point. The access point will broadcast the channel that your unit must use (and your unit will automatically accept that channel assignment). The access point will also broadcast the SSID (network identification, or "Access Point ID" as it might be called). The Setup Password in the access point should be set to "public" or "any" or whatever setting means "no password needed." Likewise, both the access point and your Wi-Fi card or USB unit must have encryption turned off. (Wi-Fi encryption doesn't do much good anyway, so if you really want to protect your data, encrypt it using other methods.)

You will be able to simply directly receive your e-mail if the computer has been using your home Internet connection in the past for e-mail. This is true, for example, for your main desktop machine.

CH
5

However, if you're adding Wi-Fi to a portable, it's likely that you will have used an 800 number connection, or otherwise made your connections from motel rooms rather than your home Internet connection. In that case, to make your portable work with your new Wi-Fi e-mail source, all you need to do to set up e-mail accounts is to run the appropriate program in the e-mail client. For example, Eudora, an e-mail application, offers a New Account Wizard. Outlook Express has an Internet Connection Wizard, which you can run by selecting Add in the Outlook Express Tools, Accounts menu option. More advanced users can enter e-mail settings directly using property dialog boxes.

IF YOU HAVE PROBLEMS

The access point will broadcast IP addresses to your USB units or PCM cards. Try running Internet Explorer (or some other browser) to see whether your Internet connection works. If you are having problems at this point, shut down Windows and reboot your computer. Also unplug your cable modem from the electric outlet and let it rest for a minute. Then replug your cable modem into the power line and let it go through its initialization process for another minute or so. After Windows reboots, see whether you can now get a connection to the Internet.

IF YOU STILL HAVE PROBLEMS

If you still cannot get multiple computers using the same access point to take advantage of your broadband connection, you may have to check with your Wi-Fi manufacturer to see whether you need additional or alternative hardware, such a residential gateway, which would broadcast multiple IP addresses. Or contact your broadband ISP to see whether there is some special requirement on their end. Beware, though, that many tech support offices will not help with internal network problems. Recall our advice: See that your Internet connection is working with one fixed computer first. That way, any problems you encounter later when adding your Wi-Fi equipment are clearly related to the Wi-Fi hardware, in which case you can call the Wi-Fi manufacturer's tech support line.

ISDN, ORDINARY PHONE LINE, OR DSL MODEM CONNECTIONS

Creating a distributed (Wi-Fi) connection to ISDN, phone line, or DSL broadband ISPs is quite similar to the cable modem connection described in detail in this chapter. Physically, there are minor differences. For example, you must purchase an access point that has a phone line style plug if you intend to connect to a phone line, or attach to a DSL modem for a DSL connection. (A DSL modem looks pretty much like a cable modem, and employs the same ethernet cable connection in back.)

In addition to the obvious physical differences, there are some other minor differences as well:

- If your LAN has a DHCP server (Dynamic Host Configuration Protocol) it means that your computers are automatically configured to use TCP/IP (Internet) connections. If that is the case, you must use the access point's setup utility software to first specify a cable modem or LAN-style connection (see Figure 5.3) *before* connecting your access point to your LAN.

- An ISDN router Internet connection is similar to a cable modem connection. You connect an ethernet cable between the ISDN router unit and your access point. You connect the ISDN unit as usual to the ISDN line jack. There is no physical connection between the computers and the ISDN unit—the computers communicate with it via the Wi-Fi access point using radio waves.

- A telephone line connection requires a special access point unit with a phone connection jack, of course, and a telephone-style cable to run between the access point and the phone jack. What's more, this specialized access point includes its own modem hardware. You are permitted to connect via Wi-Fi as many as 49 computers to this single access point modem unit, but throughput suffers. It's recommended that you limit the number of connected machines to fewer than 16.

Manufacturers differ in the capability of their hardware. For example, The ORiNOCO Residential Gateway unit offers a three-in-one capability: dialup modem and cable/DSL connectivity in one product. The primary use for the modem connection in this hardware is that you can use it if the broadband connection goes down.

- A DSL modem connection is also similar to a cable modem connection. You connect an ethernet cable between the DSL modem and your Wi-Fi access point. There is no physical connection between the computers and the DSL modem.

SHARING FILES AND RESOURCES

There are probably two primary uses for any network—wired or wireless. One is sharing an Internet connection, and the second sharing files and resources, such as printers.

In this chapter you saw how to connect an access point to various kinds of Internet connections, so the access point could broadcast that connection to as many as 49 computers (16 maximum recommended) on Sony Vaio access points.

However, after an access point is broadcasting (and receiving) radio waves to and from Wi-Fi equipped computers—why not also permit these computers to share their hard drives and peripherals, just as they would in an ordinary network?

You *can* use an access point Internet configuration to share files, printers, and other resources between the computers using the Wi-Fi LAN you have established in this chapter.

If this is the first time you've used a particular computer to connect to the outside world using Wi-Fi, follow the steps in Chapter 2 so you can share files with the other computer(s) in your Wi-Fi LAN. Also use the utility software that comes with Wi-Fi equipment to establish and test wireless communication between your computer(s).

CH

5

CHAPTER **6**

Putting an Antenna on Your Roof and Elsewhere

In this chapter

Antenna installation is both an art and a science. There's plenty of theory—fat books on the subject. But this chapter, like this book, will focus on practical solutions to Wi-Fi installation issues. We'll keep the technical details to a minimum.

Before getting into the problems in Wi-Fi LANs that antennas can solve, let's first establish a ground rule: There are no absolute rules when it comes to antenna design or placement, just as there will never be a best macaroni and cheese (although many believe that Kraft has already hit the target).

Oh, you'll find lots of people offering lots of recipes for the "best" Wi-Fi antenna and the "best" place to locate one. Go ahead and try these suggestions if you like. However, the variables of signal propagation patterns, interference, and the special needs of each Wi-Fi installation are distinctive. This means that you should simply experiment until you find the best results for *your* wireless network, remembering that the physical environment surrounding your network is, in fact, unique.

TYPES OF ANTENNAS

Microphones and loudspeakers are remarkably alike in many ways. The one makes noise, the other listens to noise—but they both involve vibrating membranes attached to electronics.

The relationship between the two main types of antennas is also alike: On one side you have receiving antennas, listening for signals. On the other side are broadcasting (transmission) antennas, sending out those signals.

However, like CB, Ham, and other communication media, Wi-Fi is bidirectional. So, a single physical antenna must often perform as both transmitter and receiver. Such hardware is called a *transceiver*. Note that Wi-Fi operates in half-duplex mode: An antenna is not called up to *simultaneously* send and transmit. Instead, the Wi-Fi unit is either sending, or transmitting, at any given time.

In the Wi-Fi world, the majority of antennas are internal: built into the access point unit, or the PCM card that slips into your portable computer. However, if you need greater range, you can add external indoor or outdoor antennas (see Figure 6.1). The average cost of an external antenna ranges from around $80 up to $200.

Some cards include a small, limp external antenna that dangles off the card, somewhat like those short wires that hang off some portable radios to improve FM reception.

Some access points, too, can be beefed up with external antennas of their own. Agere's WaveLAN Range Extender can be attached to either a card (in a desktop or portable) *or* to their WavePoint-II access point The Range Extender provides an increase in signal strength (gain) of 5 decibels (dbi) and costs around $85.

Figure 6.1
This LinkSys access point's internal antenna is, technically, also a little bit external with those rabbit ears.

Note

Technical definition: What's *dbi*? You'll see antennas advertised with various dbi specs. Antenna gain is measured by comparing your antenna to an ideal antenna, known as *isotropic*. Decibels express a *ratio* between two things (such as between signal strength and the amount of noise). Antenna gain is described in *dbi,* where the *i* stands for isotropic (the idea amount of gain). So, 5dbi is better than 2dbi.

All Wi-Fi hardware has a built-in antenna connector. For example, you simply remove a small plastic protective cap to attach the WaveLAN Range Extender antenna to one of Agere's Wi-Fi units.

If you need extreme range, manufacturers, such as ZOOM, offer antennas claiming ranges up to a mile or more (see their bidirectional yagi units). Some specialized Wi-Fi antennas are reported to provide up to *ten miles* coverage—under ideal conditions (probably like on the moon).

Сн
6

Tip

If you expect to get deeply involved with Wi-Fi, perhaps you'll want to consider getting a built-in antenna next time you buy a laptop. Perhaps. Some of the latest notebook computers come with integrated Wi-Fi electronics known as *mini-PCI chip-cards* that are embedded within the notebooks' inner workings. The antenna is sometimes sunk into the plastic surrounding the notebooks' display screens. In addition to being inherently cool, integrated portable Wi-Fi also avoids the necessity of plugging in a PCM card to your laptop.

WHAT ANTENNAS DO

The job of any antenna is to improve reception and transmission. While a signal is being broadcast, it is sent out via the antenna into the air. On the reception end, the signal is fetched from the air and pumped into the electronics of the receiver. In both cases, antennas of some kind are required.

Often, amplifiers are used to electronically boost the signal before it is sent or after it is received, but amplification is a mixed blessing. It will boost the *entire* signal, not just the information (the actual desired data). Mixed in with data is noise. This is inevitable—even in digital systems. Noise is always part of any signal and, as you probably guessed, it can be amplified along with the signal. Noise filters, autocorrelation, modulation techniques, and other attempts to remove noise from signals have achieved mixed results. If a noise is discrete and easily isolated, filtering can help. Usually, though, if you are having trouble receiving a signal, adding or improving an antenna at the broadcast end is the first step to try.

The purity of a signal is measured by the Signal-to-Noise ratio (S/N) of an electronic unit, such as an amplifier. Usually measured in decibels, the S/N ratio is calculated by dividing the signal strength by the strength of the noise. The higher the ratio, the cleaner the connection. Wireless LAN installations can be described with an S/N figure that specifies link performance.

Decibal Scale

Recall that decibels (dB) describe a ratio, often involving sound, between one value and another—such as the ratio of silence to noise when measuring the racket at an airport. Like the Richter scale, which measures earth-quake strength, the dB scale is exponential. It goes up fast: 10dB is 10 times the power, but 20dB is *100 times* stronger. DB can also be used to specify signal gain, or loss. For instance, the average indoor Wi-Fi transmitter loses about 20dB every 100 feet between itself and the receiver. This loss escalates exponentially as you increase the distance between the transmitter and receiver (now you see why the decibel scale itself is exponential).

WI-FI PROBLEMS AND CURES

The Wi-Fi radio spectrum is what technicians describe as *dirty*. By that they mean it can be polluted by unwanted signals from cordless phones, microwave sources, or other units sending off signals that compete with Wi-Fi signals.

What's more, the Wi-Fi signal is deliberately limited in power and, therefore, range. If you want to remain on the good side of the FCC you don't provide amplification or antenna boost that exceeds the legal signal strength limit. Wi-Fi units operate at less than one watt of power. Also, in a large office, more than one Wi-Fi LAN may be in operation and you don't want them interfering with each other.

Also, as many Wi-Fi enthusiasts have discovered, even something as innocent as a stack of books can interfere with signals. Technical books, especially, because (using longer words) they are on average thicker and denser.

All PC 802.11b cards have an internal (integrated) antenna, but you'll find that in some situations it simply doesn't do the job. If your PC or portable is located inside a drawer, under a desk, behind a file cabinet, next to big stacks of papers, on the wrong side of a big printer, or any other position that blocks the signal, you'll likely have reception and/or transmission problems.

If you face this kind of problem, you might want to try an outboard antenna such as the Agere's WaveLAN Range Extender (see Figure 6.2).

Figure 6.2
This indoor antenna from Agere can be used to boost signals from access points, desktop PCs, or portable PCM cards.

The Range Extender can be placed on a desk, on top of a file cabinet, or even attached to a wall or ceiling. The wall and ceiling solutions are generally used to improve the performance of an access point unit rather than a PC card.

The Range Extender's radio pattern is a pancake shape, as shown in Figure 6.3.

This antenna's performance will be degraded if you put it near metal surfaces, such as a file cabinet. Thick concrete walls and similarly thick, dense materials, such as technical books also impede performance.

CH
6

Figure 6.3
This antenna pattern
works best when the
antenna is mounted
upright.

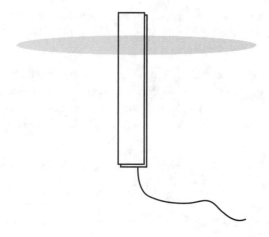

As is true with most any antenna for most any purpose, line-of-sight (unobstructed) views offer the ideal placement. If you hide the antenna behind thick stacks of magazines or any other obstruction, you're hampering the antenna's ability to do its job. Put the antenna in a good place. Remember what line-of-sight means: Think of your antenna as a bright light that you're locating in such a way that it will illuminate all the Wi-Fi card units you want it to reach. Put it in a central location, and put it as high as is practical. Is a file cabinet blocking one of the card units from "seeing" your antenna? Perhaps that cabinet can be moved.

Specifications vary, but an Agere unit we've installed here operates in the 2400 to 2500MHz range and boasts a 2.5dBi gain. This figure includes the losses incurred from the connector and the antenna cable. When comparing antenna gain, it's important that you don't compare apples to oranges. Find out whether or not the gain spec factors in the cable and connector losses.

When properly mounted, the Agere WaveLAN Range Extender should improve the range (the distance between access point and "linked" computer) by as much as 50% in an unobstructed (clear line-of-sight) pathway, such as an office filled with desks, but no cubicles or other walls. This setup assumes that if you put your head near the antenna, you could physically see the units it is intended to communicate with. (If that doesn't work, put your head next to the antenna and pretend you're a light bulb.)

In a subdivided office, you can expect as much as a 15% gain in range performance. By *subdivided*, I mean typical hollow-wall cubicles that are about five feet high.

Double these figures to 100% (unobstructed) and 30% (obstructed by cubicles) if you attach antennas on both ends of the communication link (to the access points as well as the linked computers).

IMPROVING COMMUNICATION

Some organizations, notably SFLAN discussed in Chapter 7, "Lighting Up the Neighborhood," are trying to "light up" entire cities with wireless connectivity. The idea is that you should be able to turn on your portable (computer or other device) and connect, right then and there in the park or in a chair sitting outside a café. If this noble experiment works, the Internet could become as pervasive, and inexpensive, as FM radio.

Of course, there are some stumbling blocks in the way of such free and omnipresent Wi-Fi. Impediments, such as signal strength limitations, the FCC's antenna power constraints, and the not insignificant problems associated with trying to offer for free what other people are selling.

However, no matter what your situation, at some point while using Wi-Fi (especially if you're using a laptop), you'll likely find yourself grappling with the "dirty" current bandwidth and wanting to improve your Wi-Fi communications.

One user who lives near the Lawrence Livermore Laboratory experiences significant problems from what must be top-secret escaping microwave radiation. There have been several reports that birds *fly backward* when passing over the LL Lab.

Another Wi-Fi enthusiast has problems every time his neighbor gets home from work and fires up her cordless phone. (Just kidding about the birds, but not about the Wi-Fi interference that leaks from Lawrence Livermore, or the talkative neighbor.)

In some cases, a good solution to connection interference (or simply to be able to take your portable and connect outside by the pool) is to put up a nice rooftop antenna. Just like in the old days before cable and satellite TV.

MR. TECHNO TALKS SCIENCE

Before describing how to choose, then install, an outdoor Wi-Fi antenna, I need to put on my Techno propeller hat for a few minutes and explain some of the problems you may encounter when setting up your own Wi-Fi local area network. Problems that a relatively inexpensive antenna, or other measures, can often solve.

INTERFERENCE

Wi-Fi competes with microwave ovens, elevators, some cordless phones, and a few other electronic devices for space in the 2.4GHz S Band. This interference can sometimes result in errors in data transmission, or simply slowing down the Wi-Fi communication until the delays become noticeable or even intolerable.

How do you tell that you are experiencing interference problems rather than, say, multipath distortion (described later in this chapter) or degradation of your Wi-Fi communication resulting from having the units too far apart or blocked by machinery, walls, or some other obstruction? The answer is that interference is usually *intermittent*.

Your data flows around your Wi-Fi LAN just fine most of the time, but it slows down significantly during the lunch hour (check the microwave oven in the break room). Or perhaps Wi-Fi communication is great until 9 a.m. when the sales force finishes its daily meeting and goes back to their desks and starts using their cordless phones. Does your Wi-Fi data travel fast between the patio and the main office *except in the spring and summer months?* Can you figure out why?

Bluetooth devices (used for such wireless communication as PDC connections to desktop computers) have the potential to interfere with Wi-Fi too. However, as I pointed out in Chapter 1, "Understanding Wi-Fi," the Bluetooth technology has not yet caught on with the consumer. It may never catch on. Nonetheless, if someone in your organization is using Bluetooth, it is another possible source of serious interference with Wi-Fi throughput. Interestingly, Bluetooth doesn't suffer interference from Wi-Fi because Bluetooth transmissions routinely switch frequencies within the S Band range hundreds of times more often Wi-Fi equipment does.

Tip

If you do want to combine Wi-Fi with Bluetooth in the same location, you might want to take a look at Mobilian Corporation, a company that is designing solutions to precisely this problem. It offers a product called TrueRadio, which endeavors to integrate Bluetooth and Wi-Fi systems—managing the potential interference generated by these two technologies. You can find out more about Mobilian's TrueRadio at www.mobilian.com/TrueRadio_FAQs.htm.

LOCATING THE SOURCE OF THE PROBLEM

The best way to track down the source of intermittent interference is to check transmission speed at various times during the day or week. Use the utility program that comes with Wi-Fi equipment (see Chapter 2, "Setting Up Your Personal Wireless Network") to measure throughput; check the noise level (or "strength") figure at different times. Some utility programs include a log or history feature, like the Orinoco program shown in Figure 6.4.

Try it at 7 a.m. when no one has yet arrived at work. Then test the speed (data throughput) at various times during the day. This can often help you pinpoint the culprit. Note that even though cordless phones and microwave ovens are your most likely offenders, interference on the Wi-Fi band can also come from some burglar alarm systems, street lights, elevators, copy machines, and other devices that employ radio frequency communication, either to serve their primary purpose, or simply as a byproduct of their operation. Outdoors, interference problems are usually less severe, but leaves can block signals during spring and summer. Also, pay attention to the weather report: High humidity, smog, fog, snow, rain, and smoke can all degrade Wi-Fi transmission rates.

The Spread Spectrum technology used by most radio-based products helps to alleviate interference somewhat. However, if you are experiencing interference with your Wi-Fi LAN, you might want to check first to see whether 2.4 band portable phones are in use nearby (within 100 feet), or whether a microwave oven is within 50 feet.

Figure 6.4
This program can display a graph of the noise detected over a twenty-four hour period.

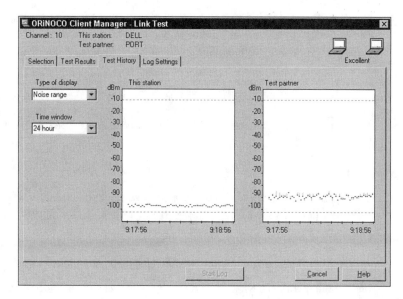

What if you are in an office building and you share a wall with a dude who is always talking on his cordless phone and messing up your Wi-Fi system? Call the FCC? No, your only recourse is to do what Martha Stewart does in these situations: get into the kitchen and *start baking muffins*! Then politely give him some muffins, and plead with your neighbor to use a different cordless phone that doesn't operate in the S Band. There is no government agency that will adjudicate Wi-Fi interference problems. Wi-Fi operates within a public license-free band. The FCC, therefore, is not required to find a solution to your problem with your neighbor. Of course, if the neighbor is *amplifying* the signal of an S Band device, that would be illegal and the FCC is likely to be interested.

The FCC's Rules: Are You Legal?

FCC rules state:

"The maximum peak output power of the intentional radiator shall not exceed the following:

(1) For frequency hopping systems operating in the 2400-2483.5 MHz or 5725–5850 MHz band and for all direct sequence systems: 1 watt."

Translated into English: *Intentional radiator* means electronics such as wireless phones and your Wi-Fi unit that send out radio waves on purpose to accomplish their job, as opposed to an *unintentional* radiator, such as a microwave oven that doesn't really *want* to radiate, but sort of leaks waves while trying to do some unrelated job such as defrosting. (The FCC prefers to call transmission antennas *radiators*.) *Frequency hopping* refers to a spread spectrum technology used to reduce interference during Wi-Fi and cordless phone communications. *2400–2483.5MHz* is the band allocated to Wi-Fi and other equipment. 1 watt is very little power; think of light bulbs' wattage.

The FCC goes on to deal with the gain in signal strength achieved when you attach an antenna:

CH
6

"Systems operating in the 2400–2483.5 MHz band that are used exclusively for fixed, point-to-point operations may employ transmitting antennas with directional gain greater than 6 dBi provided the maximum peak output power of the intentional radiator is reduced by 1 dB for every 3 dB that the directional gain of the antenna exceeds 6 dBi."

Put another way: If you need a strong gain, get a technician to certify that you are not violating this FCC rule, whatever it might mean. Figuring out if you're breaking the antenna laws requires some complex measurements: You have to factor in the losses caused by the cable between the transmitter and the antenna, the true maximum directional gain of your antenna, interference with other antennas (such as polarization) and associated specs.

MULTIPATH LOSS

One difficulty that Wi-Fi manufacturers must wrestle with is called multipath loss. This problem isn't unique to Wi-Fi; it has been bedeviling television signals for over 50 years. The difficulty is this: A signal goes out in many directions from a transmitting antenna. Some of the signal goes directly in a straight line to the receiving antenna, but other versions of the signal arrive *later*, after bouncing off walls, desks, and other surfaces.

So, one problem you face when installing a Wi-Fi antenna is to find the right balance. There is a tradeoff between providing enough gain (improvement in signal strength) to make communications within your LAN effective, without providing so much gain that you generate significant multipath loss.

The receiver is thus getting the same signal, but arriving at different times—like many rapid-fire echoes. This is similar to the way a singer's voice becomes less clear in a room with "live" (highly reflective) acoustics. The sound reverberates. That's why professional recording studios cover their walls with special soft, absorbent acoustic material. Amateur studios line the walls and ceiling with shag carpet, which does the job, even though it looks really bad.

Humans can usually understand the lyrics even in live rooms because our brains can compensate for quite a bit of reverb. We're the *psycho* in psychoacoustics.

Likewise, using electronic tricks such as equalization, manufacturers attempt to reduce multipath interference. But if you find your Wi-Fi installation bedeviled by poor reception, remember that one cure might be to deaden the environment.

Carpet, fabric-covered dividers, and certain kinds of ceiling tile are highly absorbent and can effectively reduce multipath problems. In fact, many of the measures taken to reduce ordinary noise in a room also serve to reduce multipath problems.

You can also consider adding more access points to decrease the distance between transmission sources. Another solution is known as *antenna diversity*, which means employing two or more antennas with somewhat uncorrelated signals at the same time. Manufacturers building equipment with antenna diversity can use electronics to dynamically switch between the antennas, depending on which one has the best signal at any given time.

Multipath distortion is rarely a problem outdoors, at least in the Wi-Fi band.

GAIN

The gain of an antenna describes how much amplification the antenna provides—how much the antenna boosts the signal—and consequently how much further the signal can travel and be used for communication. Gain is related to the propagation pattern. There are many variations in antenna design, but there are only two primary antenna types: omnidirectional and directional.

Omnidirectional antennas radiate in all directions, like a sphere (at least that's the ideal), but have the least gain. Directional antennas focus their signal in one direction, in a pattern that is often football-shaped, with one point of the football touching each of two communicating directional antennas. This pattern is known as the *fresnel* zone.

As a general rule, omnidirectional antennas are used indoors and directional antennas are used outside. Also, snap-on or dipole antennas are suitable for laptops and other portable Wi-Fi units. High-gain antennas are usually employed to boost signal for access points. These antennas are usually placed on a wall or roof and require a fairly long connection cable between the access point hardware and the antenna itself.

GETTING CONNECTED

The FCC requires that every Wi-Fi manufacturer provide a connector for an external antenna on all its cards and access point units. So you can be sure there is a place to connect to; you just have to figure out *where*. There is no agreed-upon standard for these connections; they are proprietary. Cisco and LinkSys use a reverse TNC connector; Avaya employs a tiny plug of their own design; Intel hardware has a reverse BNC connector. ORiNOCO units are also proprietary.

The same companies that make Wi-Fi hardware manufacture some external antennas. Agere, for instance, offers a large choice, including small portable antennas, a 5dbi omnidirectional vehicle antenna, a 10dbi omnidirectional base station antenna, and a 24dbi parabolic grid antenna. However, antennas have been designed and manufactured for many decades, so there are lots of sources.

AN "N" CONNECTOR AT THE ANTENNA END

CH
6

Most antennas employ what is called the standard "N" connector. They look somewhat like the connectors used with cable TV coax wire. In fact, you'll want to use coaxial cable for any antenna connection that is greater than a few feet. Try to get cable that has the correct N connectors already installed, and ready to attach to the antenna you purchase. You don't want to be bothered learning the art and science of attaching coax cable to connectors.

The coax cable N connector is male and the connector on the antenna is female.

With any outdoor antenna, it is wise to install a lightning arrestor. Also, speaking of lightning, don't try to install the antenna during a storm—even if the storm is 10 miles off. Lightning can travel far and fast, and it likes nothing more than finding someone up on a roof, looking up at the sky, holding an antenna in his hand. Lightning arrestors are designed to prevent your card or access point from getting fried if lightning hits your antenna. Note that lightning arrestors connect in a single direction. So check the documentation, or the instructions printed on the arrestor itself, to ensure that you know which end is supposed to point toward the antenna. Although lightning arrestors are highly recommended, grounding an antenna is required by law. Specifically, the National Electrical Code—not to mention common sense—insists on grounding every external antenna.

A PIGTAIL AT THE WI-FI END

To connect the antenna cable to your Wi-Fi unit, you need what they call a *pigtail*. This is a coupler with your Wi-Fi unit's (probably proprietary) antenna socket connector on one end and the standard N connector to attach to the antenna cable on the other end.

TUNING YOUR ANTENNA

Whether you put up one or several, indoors or outdoors, you'll likely want to test your antenna to find the best place to position it, and in the case of directional antennas, the best bearing to point it in.

Tuning a Wi-Fi antenna is not difficult, although the job is easier if there are two people. One person stands next to the antenna and rotates (or moves it around to different locations) while the other person holds a portable computer (or whatever target unit's reception you want to test). The portable runs the utility software that came with your Wi-Fi hardware, noting changes in signal strength caused by the repositioning of the antenna. If you've ever assisted in the installation of a TV or satellite antenna, you know the routine. There will likely be one position or orientation that produces noticeably the best results. This "sweet spot" is particularly noticeable with directional antennas, but even omnidirectional indoor antennas can suddenly surge in effectiveness if you lift them above a file cabinet, for example, which was blocking the signal.

As you can see in Figure 6.5, utility software provides useful statistics about both the strength of a signal, as well as the noise attacking that signal.

Figure 6.5
Watch both signal strength and noise levels while repositioning an antenna to find the best site.

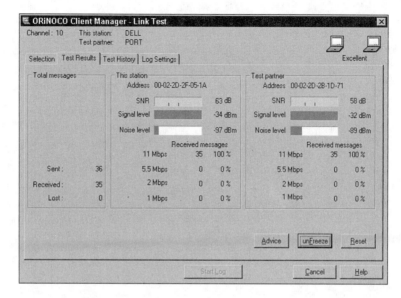

WHERE TO GO FROM HERE

We've covered the essentials of Wi-Fi antenna installation. However, anyone who knows a Ham radio devotee or shortwave radio enthusiast has likely noticed that the subject of antennas is deep and vast. There is a huge body of science and literature on this topic. Many people love to experiment with placement and different antenna designs—both commercial and homemade.

If you are interested in exploring antenna theory further, the Internet, of course, offers a wealth of ideas. Use the Google search engine and look for *wireless network antenna*, *Wi-Fi antenna*, and similar targets. Also check out Ham radio organizations and publications.

Additional information about antennas can be found elsewhere in this book as well. Using multiple antennas is explored in Chapter 3, "Larger Scale Wi-Fi Setups" and becoming your own Wi-Fi cell is covered in Chapter 7.

CH

6

Lighting Up the Neighborhood

In this chapter

This chapter contains two case studies that illustrate how to light up a neighborhood or campus—providing Wi-Fi coverage (and by extension, an Internet connection) throughout a large area. Fabled Wake Forest University in North Carolina has one of the most extensive wireless networks of any educational institution. And, as usual, San Francisco proves *avant-garde*. That beautiful city is home of SFLAN, one of the first and most successful Wi-Fi people-power community networks. Here are the people who have built these networks, and this is their story.

CASE STUDY: SFLAN—"UNWIRING" THE PRESIDIO

One of the most influential 802.11b community networks is SFLAN, the brainchild of Internet entrepreneur Brewster Kahle and Harvie Branscomb . Branscomb has also been instrumental in setting up the Aspen, Colorado valley with an 802.11b wireless network.

Kahle is the founder of Alexa Internet, a company whose technology is used in making it easier to retrieve information on the Web. (You can see some of the Alexa technology if you are running Internet Explorer by selecting Show Related Links from the Tools menu.)

Alexa, which is now owned by Amazon.com, also runs a Web bot that is involved in archiving the entire Web, a process that will, according to Kahle, create the largest library of knowledge in human history. "The last time this was attempted," he says, "was the Alexandrian library of Ptolemy, and then we were talking about 5,000 scrolls."

It's clear that Brewster Kahle likes to think big. So, why the SFLAN project? "By setting up our local community for wireless access we were hoping to jump-start Moore's law for communications, and get people thinking so that the same economies of scale that came into play with microprocessors could become effective here," Kahle states.

THE SFLAN GEOGRAPHY

As a test case, SFLAN has successfully 802.11b-enabled San Francisco's Presidio. The Presidio is a part of the 74,000-acre Golden Gate National Recreation Area. The Presidio Trust manages 80% of the Presidio land; the coastal areas comprising the remaining 20% are managed by the National Park Service.

A former army base, the Presidio is now a community where artists live and work, and is home to museums and experimental ventures.

SFLAN has placed wireless access points within the Presidio in schools, a laundry, a firehouse, coffee shops, homes and offices, and in the Exploratorium, a world-famous educational museum for children.

LOGGING ON TO SFLAN

To log on to the Internet using the SFLAN network, within the Presidio neighborhood, simply open your Web browser. You may also have to set the Network Name (SSID) to PRESIDO.

It's worth noting that SFLAN is entirely free; unlike the MobileStar or Wayport networks, money is not charged for usage, and there is no access control.

THE SFLAN PHILOSOPHY

SFLAN is a prototype for a future "free" wireless world that bypasses the traditional telco cell phone and wireline providers. According to the SFLAN manifesto (`http://www.sflan.com`):

Imagine a citywide wireless LAN that grows from an anarchistic cooperation:

> "From a laptop in any park, from a PC in any house, from any handheld assistant on the street, you can get at the Internet at blazing speed. From there, imagine a phone that uses your base station when you are in your house but uses the Net when you are out of range…"

> "The idea is to use miniature radio beacons to build a citywide LAN that runs at megabits/second. Every time someone's local network is connected to SFLAN, then everyone in the surrounding blocks can also connect. At different points, this wireless traffic is put on the Internet backbone."

In other words, the world that SFLAN contemplates is an extension of the worldview that was prevalent in the early adoption of the Internet. To make the SFLAN vision a reality, a great many individual users, small businesses, and organizations would have to make their wireless networks available on an ad-hoc basis.

THE FUTURE OF SFLAN

SFLAN was built in the late 1990s to prove that a neighborhood *could* be connected via wireless technology—and that point has been proved. The question is, what next?

Brewster Kahle believes that the future of wireless technologies such as 802.11 is "just awesome."

"We're all using cordless phones," he says. "I carry a cell phone, and use a cordless in my office. Why should these devices be 802.11 enabled? It's just a matter of time.

"The 2.4 Gigahertz spectrum is like an anarchistic wildlife park. It's mayhem. What we need is a spectrum devoted to the public interest, but with rules. Instead of seeking to make profit, the FCC ought to seek to have spectrums used and regulated in the public interest— in much the way there are rules of the road.

"We also need higher power access points. Current equipment, with power ratings in the 30–100 milli-Watt range typically goes a few hundred feet. When this is boosted to one Watt, one hundred or so access points would be enough to network an entire area the size of San Francisco. To grab a signal, you'd just need to put a repeater on your roof. Many distant parts of the world could be connected this way.

"Once I have my computer always with me, and always connected, applications can be Web-based (rather than copied locally). My calendar and address book become communication tools rather than static repositories.

CH

7

"PDAs like Visors equipped with 802.11b and cameras are great two-way communication tools. School kids can use them to get feedback from teachers. If you are taking a tour of the forest, and want to learn more about a particular moss, or if you are at the seashore and find a starfish, you can use your wireless devices to get remote experts to explain these things to you."

"Ubiquitous wireless networking is the greatest tool for communication and education there is. But don't look to the phone companies to bring it to us. Instead, we have to figure out how to push the envelope in the way SFLAN did, and create grass roots wireless networks of greater and greater utility."

WAKE FOREST LIGHTS UP

Leafy Wake Forest University has something more to recommend it than quality professors, world-class athletics, and a lovely campus. Since March 2000, the students and faculty have benefited from one of the most extensive wireless networks in the country. It's not completely "free" like SFLAN, but it's pretty inexpensive and it covers the whole campus.

Jay Dominick, Wake Forest's Assistant VP for Information Systems, is very happy with its choice of systems. Early on they determined that they wanted to avoid worrying about the engineering problems of overlapping, conflicting access points, and radio frequency interference (from sources such as portable phones, Bluetooth, and the microwave ovens used nonstop by students cooking up Ramen Noodle soup snacks). So, they chose 802.11 wireless technology rather than the newer, faster 802.11b equipment.

However, the differences between the two technologies are not profound, as you'll see. Both Microsoft and Stanford selected 802.11b, so you'll find proponents of either variant of the 802.11 standard. Ultimately, nearly everyone will migrate to the next generation 802.11a standard anyway, for the usual reason: greater throughput.

TWO PLUSSES, TWO MINUSES

One drawback of 802.11 is that the equipment can cost more than equivalent 802.11b units. (The Wake Forest 802.11 access points are under $1,000 versus 11b's under $200; 802.11 PCM cards for portables are under $300 versus 11b's under $100.) A second drawback is that 802.11 is slower: Rated at 2Mbps, the average true throughput is around 1Mbps. This compares to 11b's claimed 11Mbps, and true throughput average of around 4Mpbs.

But there are plusses as well. The advantages of the 802.11 standard are twofold: It uses frequency hopping (FHSS) rather than 11b's DSSS technology. This means that you can install access points anywhere, without worrying about assigning correct channels (see Chapter 3, "Larger Scale Wi-Fi Setups"). With FHSS, no channels are required. Second, there's no interference to worry about from portable phones or other devices that share the 802.11 bandwidth.

Jay Dominic points out that he's glad he doesn't have to worry about allocating channels. You can just put up access point units anywhere you want without concern about interference between the units. Frequency hopping "splatters your packets all over the spectrum. It's using that entire spectrum instead of just one chunk of it."

Why, then, didn't the 11b standard incorporate frequency hopping? Because it isn't capable of accommodating 11b's faster data rates.

Frequency hopping modulates the data signal with a carrier that leaps rapidly from frequency to frequency. This constant hopping makes it unlikely that narrowband interference signals will coincidentally use the same frequency at the same time as the hopper. About as likely as swatting a fly with a finger. But how does the PCM card in the user's portable know which frequencies to tune to, and in what order? Both access point and PCM card share a "hopping code," a list of the frequencies.

More than 79 different frequencies are employed during a frequency hopping transmission, but the time spent using any particular frequency is only .04 second. Then the next hop occurs. What's more, if any interference is detected during the transmission of a packet of data, the packet is retransmitted on the next frequency in the sequence.

The next generation of Wi-Fi (802.11a) will use yet another modulation technology: orthogonal frequency division multiplexing (OFDM). It gets superior results, dealing quite effectively with both multipath and RF interference. Most important: It is capable of higher throughput than either DSSS or FHSS. See the glossary at the end of this book for more details about DSSS and FHSS.

COVERING THE CAMPUS

The goal at Wake Forest was to virtually blanket the entire campus. A wired LAN was already operating, and even today there are outlets scattered all over campus where students can directly plug in to the wired LAN for the highest possible data speeds.

There are currently 150 wireless access points, lighting up nearly every corner of the Wake Forest campus. They are installed everywhere—in almost all public areas including most residence halls, throughout the cafeteria, in some classrooms, most outdoor areas where students are likely to be, such as the quad, and the many grassy hillocks where students enjoy impromptu picnics amid the twittering bluebirds and the fragrance of the old magnolia trees.

It only took the university about two months to get its original allotment of 120 access points up and broadcasting. Happily, there were no unpleasant surprises during the installation. They had correctly anticipated that they would need more access points in the older buildings with their thick, masonry walls. Radio signals just don't go through that kind of wall very well at all. However, modern construction practices employ thin walls and drop ceilings— both of which permit relatively easy radio frequency penetration. The average coverage area for an access point at Wake Forest is a 100–125 feet radius. It drops off, though, when those thick older walls are in the way.

CH

7

"We were surprised how much it did cover. The signal will bounce down a stairwell; we didn't think that would happen. We were pretty pleased with how the coverage worked. The site survey built in a fair bit of leeway. The survey engineers were pretty conservative when estimating the number of access points we would need, and their range," says Dominick.

The university is continually expanding the coverage by adding new access points. They also employ three different kinds of antennas: pipe antennas, small cell phone-like antennas, and patch antennas. Each offers different coverage patterns. Which style they choose depends on the special requirements of each location.

What About the Costs?

The university rents PCM cards to the students for $200 per year, which is pretty reasonable considering that they get Internet services as well. This fee is about what most people pay for ordinary phone modem Internet access.

The university leases its hardware from Symbol Technologies. The cost of installing each access point can range anywhere from $50 to $500 depending on the difficulty of hanging the unit. For example, one access point is way up high on the wall of an atrium. Power and data were run up there, and just physically attaching the little access point unit to the wall required the services of a crane. This was one of the $500 jobs.

Ongoing maintenance? Virtually zero. For one thing, there are few access points attached outside where weather, and all those bluebirds, could damage them. To provide outside coverage, an access point unit is attached to a wall safely inside a building. Then an antenna is attached and pointed through a nearby window. Thus even some of the antennas stay warm and dry inside the walls.

The Internet and Free Files

Wake Forest's Internet connection provides a theoretical blazing 125Mbps throughput—about 100 times faster than cable modem. (Typical maximum cable modem transmission speed averages around 1.3Mbps.)

But that 125Mbps connection of course remains theoretical. Several factors slow down the throughput to what Jay Dominick estimates is a pretty sluggish actual Internet connection speed over their wireless LAN. Like most universities, Wake Forest has "had such a terrible time with Morpheus [and other such sharing applications] that the actual bandwidth that a student is getting is actually less than a modem at this point." In other words, less than 52K.

That's why the students still attach their computers to the wire LAN plugs available all over campus. Attached to the wire LAN they can get up to 10Mbps throughput.

Media Orders of Magnitude

Consider the interesting way that various media form an order of magnitude stairstep pattern. Easiest to store and transmit is text; it requires very little bandwidth. Three minutes worth of reading material—about 1,600 words—can be stored in about 10,000 bytes (10K).

A couple of orders of magnitude up from text sits pictures: A single, one-megapixel photo uses up around 600K. Next higher is music: Radiohead's *Creep* is a three-minute song and, compressed in the MP3 format, needs about 3,300K storage. Up at the top of the stairs is video, moving pictures, the equivalent of flipping 24 still photos past our eyes per second. Three minutes of AVI video requires around 665,000K storage.

You see the problem: Many college students are enthusiastic about "sharing" music and movies. Co-eds use the Internet to trade entertainment. Napster started it all, forming thousands of simultaneous pipelines between users' hard drives all over the world. But, as you've seen, music eats up far less bandwidth than videos. Now that Napster is down for the count, today's students seem to be focusing on video. "The new technologies are all about video. If you can imagine the difference between listening to a song and watching a full length feature film and the bandwidth differences therein."

Benign Uses

Of course campus life isn't simply one, big, nonstop MPEG movie festival, plus picnics. A typical student sitting in the library might have e-mail and instant messaging up and running, along with the library catalog and windows displaying course material that professors have made available. In fact, instant messaging is so popular that it eclipses cell phone usage in many cases.

Connecting to the university's wireless LAN requires no intervention by the user. When you press the On button to activate your portable computer while on campus, your wireless PCM card instantly seeks out the best available access point, communicates with it briefly, sends a password, then connects to the university LAN. Load-balancing technology automatically chooses the access point currently bearing the least amount of traffic.

Nor is encryption an issue in this idyllic campus setting either. Data encryption is simply not employed at all, and the only authentication process involves that secret password stored in the firmware of the PCM cards and the access points. Obviously, this system isn't terribly secure, but Dominick points out that the wireless LAN "hasn't been a security issue for us."

As you can see, the wireless LAN is a great success at Wake Forest. It continues to add access points and expects to "gently migrate" to 802.11a technology over the next few years. The migration will be gentle because the current 802.11 or 802.11b units and their 802.11a successors do not interfere with each other whatsoever.

Of course the new 11a technology will be many times faster than current wireless LANs. It's likely, though, that a kind of bandwidth Peter Principle will kick in when the throughput speeds up. Streaming video, anyone?

CH

7

CHAPTER 8

SECURITY AND ENCRYPTION

In this chapter

No security system is impermeable. The goal of computer security is to allow you, and others who have permission and can be trusted, to get through the security wall, while also keeping unauthorized people out.

However, simply because *you* can permeate it, the wall is, by definition, permeable. If intruders can figure out the steps you take to get through, they can then imitate those steps. They can pose as you and just walk right in.

SPECIAL WI-FI SECURITY ISSUES

Wireless communication suffers from a special security problem: There is no physical barrier to the interception of the signals. Wi-Fi units broadcast RF signals, radio frequency. Anyone with some (not very advanced) knowledge of security technology, and a Wi-Fi PCI card stuck into his or her portable, can waltz past your offices, sit down on a bus stop bench, and, potentially at least, tap into your Wi-Fi access point.

There are some safeguards built in to wire networks that Wi-Fi LAN members can also employ. These include drive, file and folder permissions (or the denial thereof); user and group accounts; auditing, password requirements; Group Policies; and specifying various levels of "user rights." (See Chapter 2, "Setting Up Your Personal Wireless Network," for additional information about these measures.)

But by far your best protection against the shifty looking guy on the bus stop bench is *encryption*. After all, if he's sitting out there intercepting your RF broadcast messages, he doesn't have to worry about permissions, logon names, operating system passwords, and all the rest of it. Most of those features merely thwart people who are already in the building, who are actually allowed on the LAN, but aren't given total access to everything on it.

You should think of your Wi-Fi communications as having the same level of vulnerability as communications sent over the Internet. In other words: complete vulnerability to interception and viewing.

A less frequent, but potentially equally damaging problem, is someone who intercepts, then adds to or modifies, your data. This is part of what's called the *authentication* issue. Modified data can cause serious disruptions. For example, banks transfer billions of dollars a day. If someone substitutes his bank account number for the intended recipient's number, millions might be dumped into the wrong account. And by the time the deception is discovered, the thief has long since moved the money to an untraceable offshore account.

The NT and Windows 2000 NTFS hard drive technology include encryption capabilities so you can scramble individual files. In addition, Wi-Fi includes two built-in security measures: traditional encryption of the broadcast messages, and a way of smearing the radio signal called *spread spectrum*. Most experts, though, do not feel that these measures are, how shall we put it, sufficient (some experts are less diplomatic).

For example, the spread spectrum technology built into all Wi-Fi hardware is easily defeated by any but the most-rank amateur spy. SS technology does, though, help to improve signal to noise ratios, so it is employed primarily to make Wi-Fi less vulnerable to interference. As encryption, it's of little real use.

CH
8

Spread Spectrum Technology

Wi-Fi uses Direct Sequence Spread Spectrum (DSSS) technology. DSSS modulates the RF signal and spreads the transmission over the entire frequency band allocated for Wi-Fi communication.

DSSS adds a redundant pattern to each bit that is transmitted. This pattern is called a *chip*. The precise code used to generate these chips is kept secret, in theory, from anyone other than the authorized sender and receiver hardware (users are not involved in this automatic encryption process). However, outsiders can rather easily crack this primitive security scheme. The actual value of adding this redundant code is that the chip contains enough information about the original bits that those bits can be reconstructed should they be dropped or mangled during transmission. Put another way: Adding DSSS is a way of coping with environments suffering from noise and interference, so having to retransmit dropped bits can be avoided.

Most Wi-Fi security measures are not fundamentally different from the measures that must be taken to protect a wired LAN. In fact, Wi-Fi equipment manufacturers and standards committees have come up with a system that claims to offer *wired equivalent privacy* called *WEP*. Wi-Fi also includes two additional built-in security measures: a simple access point logon Service Set Identifier (SSID) and Media Access Control (MAC) address filtering (also used on many traditional networks). Does WEP and these other techniques do the job? Unfortunately, no. See the section "Problems with WEP" later in this chapter.

Access Point SSIDs, while not as visible to intruders as the street address painted on the front door of your office, don't offer much protection. It's easy to get a SSID, but we won't describe how.

MAC is also relatively easily penetrated. Also, it wastes lots of time. The network administrator must program each access point by hand, specifying the list of MAC client computers that you permit into your LAN. Each client (laptop or desktop) that you want to permit to connect to your Wi-Fi LAN via an access point unit is identified by the unique MAC address of its USB or PCM plug in Wi-Fi card. The network administrator must therefore maintain an up-to-date list of these MAC numbers and reprogram all the access points as often as required. Needless to say, this is an impossible task for larger Wi-Fi LANs. Many access point units themselves impose an upper limit of 255 permitted client addresses; you are not allowed to program in any more than that.

MAC, SSID, and WEP technologies are optional; many network administrators simply turn them off. If you do want to employ SSID, be sure to turn off its "broadcast" feature. For obvious reasons—we can say no more.

Among other topics, in this chapter we'll explore the most common weaknesses associated with network security in general, and Wi-Fi LANs in particular. Then we'll offer our recommendations on how to avoid these weaknesses and improve your Wi-Fi security.

THE PROPRIETARY SOLUTION

Note that you can go proprietary. In other words, you can boost the security of your Wi-Fi installation if you are willing to give up flexibility. If you want specially protected roaming technologies, proprietary encryption, specialized authentication methods, semi-automatic key management, and other security features, you can find a vendor that sells these enhancements to Wi-Fi standards. But that's precisely the problem: Your equipment and its software will no longer be standard Wi-Fi machinery, so you then must then buy all your Wi-Fi units from the same vendor. But the real problem with proprietary security solutions is that your portable becomes (probably) incompatible with other Wi-Fi–enabled environments, such as airports, coffee shops, hotels, and others described in Chapter 4,"At Home and At Work," and elsewhere in this book.

Anyone setting up a security system must always try to find the best compromise between freedom and security. Nice retired people all over the country face this tradeoff. They paid off their mortgage, but they now have a much lower monthly income. They're forced to stay in their house because they cannot afford a better house, and because their house is not worth very much any more anyway. Why? Because in the 30 years they've lived there, the neighborhood has collapsed. The once-pleasant, tree-lined area has become a crack house slum, littered with abandoned cars and gunfire in the night.

What can they do? After getting robbed a few times, many decide to put bars up on all their windows. This has the obvious drawback of preventing them from getting out easily in case of fire. But they're more afraid of the crackheads breaking in than they are of fire. After all, fire is relatively rare; but nearly every night the living dead can be heard tap, tap, tapping on their windows, trying to find a way in. So the old people deal as best they can with the paradox inherent in securing walls: Make them too strong, and you imprison whatever is within.

ENCRYPTION WORKS BEST

By far the best Wi-Fi communications protection, probably the only real protection against a sophisticated intruder, is encryption. But encryption is difficult to implement: You have to manage *keys*. And, worse that that, people must be involved in their use. As we'll see, this causes even encryption to sometimes fail as a defense against motivated spies. With today's computer-versus-computer encryption/decryption warfare, you can't even count on many encryption schemes.

PROBLEMS WITH WEP

At Black Hat Briefings, a recent hacker convention in Las Vegas, Tim Newsham, a researcher at @Stake, a security company, said that the 64-bit key used in many home wireless networks can be cracked in less than a minute. Cisco Systems's Aironet 340 Series Client Adapters feature WEP (the 802.11 encryption protocol) options ranging from no WEP option at all, up to 128-bit protection.

Who would want the "no WEP option?" I don't know about *you* and your friends, but some of my friends' home family networks work just fine without any Top Security safety measures. My friends just use their little LAN to share a printer, files, and their cable modem Internet connection. Their personal lives and Web surfing are not all that explosive, so they simply do not need protection against outsiders. They're not doing anything particularly secret or particularly valuable with their computers.

Businesses, though, are often another story. To get the best current WEP security, you'd want more bits in your key. However, even the superior 128-bit key employed by some Wi-Fi LAN equipment is vulnerable to what are called *dictionary attacks*—running through a list of commonly chosen passwords until one of them works. We'll look at this kind of brute force attack shortly.

Wi-Fi's WEP encryption is based on the so-called RC4 cipher. Cryptologists have found that there are multiple weaknesses in this cipher, not least of which is the recently reported fact that easily obtained "promiscuous network" programs can quite rapidly figure out a 40-bit WEP security key and thus gain complete access to the Wi-Fi network's data. The security can be cracked in less than 15 minutes. Use a stronger 128-bit key? It takes only about 45 minutes to crack.

Tip

When we say "easily obtained" do you know what we mean? You do if you use the Internet and if you're familiar with Google, probably the best Internet search engine.

Another WEP weakness is that a static (unchanging) key is used. All it takes is a single security lapse (an intruder getting hold of a single laptop will do it), and the whole organization's Wi-Fi communications are breached.

Why was a weak 40-bit encryption built into the IEEE 802.11 specification in the first place? Answer: When the Wi-Fi specs were originally defined, 40 bits was the maximum permitted by law.

Theoretically you should attempt to secure your Wi-Fi communications just as fully as you secure your wired network, if you have one. The walls of an office containing a wired network are studded with jacks that people can plug into to join the network. So, these connections are defended by all the traditional measures: keys or passwords, special badges, pushbutton door locks, guards at the doors, and whatever. This particular layer of protection—the physical barrier—is of no use when your Wi-Fi LAN is activated: That guy on the bench outside is "inside" already. It's important that a corporate network administrator responsible for installing a Wi-Fi LAN be sure to isolate the access point units from the wired internal private network. And this isolation should include authenticating users who attempt to go across an access point from the outside to gain entrance to the wired network and, therefore, the computers in your organization.

TECHNICAL DETAILS

If you are deeply, almost suspiciously, interested in computer security like the authors of this book, you'll want to read more about the technical reasons that WEP fails to provide strong security. Read all about it at these sites:

www.isaac.cs.berkeley.edu/isaac/wep-draft.pdf

www.isaac.cs.berkeley.edu/isaac/wep-faq.html

www.cs.umd.edu/~waa/wireless.html

You'll read the details about the terrible truth: How WEP can cave from statistical analysis, tricking access points, and dictionary-building techniques.

Don't despair, though. There are solutions that will provide protection. Authenticators such as RADIUS (Remote Authentication Dial-In User Service); firewalls; VPN (Virtual Private Network); and above all, educating your personnel about the rules of good security—these are your best protections. Just don't rely on Wi-Fi's built-in security. Unless, of course, you have nothing to hide. Actually, even if privacy isn't important to you, it's nonetheless essential to use firewalls and other security measures. There are nasty viruses, denial-of-service worms, and other critters that can get into your computer and cause problems. So do be sure to protect your Wi-Fi LAN.

SOME STEPS TO TAKE

Although you cannot guarantee security, you *can* put some stumbling blocks in the way of attempted intrusions. WECA—the Wireless Ethernet Compatibility Alliance, that acts as a standards and governing body for Wi-Fi, suggests these security measures:

- Never tell anyone the key, and ensure that all your co-workers obey this fundamental rule, too.
- Avoid using a static key. Change the key often, even though that's inconvenient. This way you limit the amount of information a listener can gather if security is breached.
- Use firewalls.
- Check your Wi-Fi LAN often to see that there are no "extra" connections that cannot be accounted for. (There is utility software that can identify rogue connections, which, sometimes, are accidentally established by regular employees. Other times, these "extra connections" are outsiders listening in. See "Snorters, Sniffers, and Peekers" later in this chapter.)

To this list we would add: Take advantage of Virtual Private Networking, described in a following section "The VPN Solution."

THE PROBLEM WITH PEOPLE

Notice the first item in the previous list. It's important to realize that encryption experts often claim that by far the greatest weakness in any security system is the people who use it. To understand this problem, you have to understand a little about passwords and why they cause so many security breaches.

PASSWORD PROTECTION FLAWS

Hackers use various tactics to get into a network. One of their favorites is called the *brute force attack*, and the dictionary attack falls into this category.

The best password is as long as possible and contains digits as well as alphabetic characters. This is why most banks, and many other organizations are now insisting that "your password must be longer than six characters and must contain a digit."

Passwords are, unfortunately, often rather predictable because people make them up—and most people have both a relatively poor memory and relatively little imagination. Therefore, most passwords are short and simple. People use their dog's name, their own first name, their favorite color, and even the word *password* as their password. Whatever. Left to their own choice, people almost always choose words instead of numbers.

Words are not good passwords (the dictionary attack relies on this fact). Numbers are composed of the 10 digits. Importantly, the frequency of these digits is completely flat—you will not find any particular digit or combination of digits appearing any more often than any other digit or combination (222 is as likely as 937). With words, though, there are those striking clusters, high-frequency words or letter-combinations such as *th*, which appears in over 6% of the words used in common American English communication. Compare that to combinations like *uu*, which only appears once in the entire language, in the bizarro word *vacuum*.

Table 8.1 shows how predictable letters, syllables, and words are in English. This predictability is the basis of the dictionary attack.

TABLE 8.1	FREQUENCIES IN AMERICAN ENGLISH		
Letter	**2-Letter Groups**	**3-Letter Groups**	**Complete Words**
E (13%)	TH (3%)	THE (5%)	THE (6.5%)
T (9%)	IN (1.5%)	ING (1.5%)	OF (4%)
O (8%)	ER (1.3%)	AND (1%)	AND (3.1%)
A (7.8%)	RE (1.3%)	ION (1%)	TO (2.3%)
N (7.2%)	AN (1%)	ENT (.98%)	A (2%)
I (7%)	HE (1%)	FOR (.76%)	IN (1.77%)

The average person can't remember more than the seven digits in a phone number, and has trouble with seven. So, passwords are usually words, and short words at that. If you're in charge of administrating security at a Wi-Fi installation, your first and most important job, after installing firewalls, is to enforce strict password rules: make them long, use some digits, and don't write the password on a Post-It Note and stick it on your office wall.

SOCIAL ENGINEERING

People sometimes even use their own last name as their password! It doesn't take a master criminal to get the last names of the people working in an office. There are ways. Lots of ways.

Social engineering means security breaches that involve charming or tricking people rather than using hardware or software hacking approaches. Social engineering techniques include posing as a superior from the head office, the FBI, a field service technician with an urgent situation, and so on. Social engineering is the single most effective security penetration technique. You can put a computer inside a sealed room with 10-foot thick concrete walls, but if an employee who knows the logon sequence is chatty, lonely, or otherwise pliable, 50-foot walls would not secure the system. Security is made up of a chain of connected elements: firewalls, passwords, shredders, alarm systems, secure rooms, and so on. But the old adage applies: The security chain is only as strong as its weakest link. And all too often that weak link is a person.

SNORTERS, SNIFFERS, AND PEEKERS

If you are interested in testing your Wi-Fi installation to see how permeable, or secure, it is, consider the following products.

AIRSNORT

AirSnort isn't really a *product*. Its creators released it to the public for altruistic reasons. It's really a clever wakeup call to those who trust WEP with their private information. Here's how the authors describe AirSnort:

> "We felt that the only proper thing to do was to release the project. It is not obvious to the layman or the average administrator how vulnerable 802.11b is to attack. With huge corporations pushing it, it's easy to trust WEP; conversely, it's hard to digest a mathematical paper describing intimate details of encryption algorithms. Yes, AirSnort can be used as a cracking tool, but it can also be used to settle arguments over the safety of WEP. People with neither the inclination nor the ability to digest the papers about WEP's security can easily wrap their minds around a tool like WEP. If it took us so little time to write AirSnort, it would take a determined adversary a similarly short amount of time to develop an attacking tool. The only sane assumption to make is that a malicious hacker would have developed a tool like this."

AirSnort sits there passively listening to transmissions, like the fabled Red Lady in the café who lingers over her drinks, heavy eyeliner, smart silk gown, just happening to overhear conversations among soldiers hour after hour.

If AirSnort listens to your broadcasts long enough, it overhears enough packets to figure out your 128-bit WEP encryption key. How long? It needs to hear between 100 megabytes to 1 gigabyte of your data, and it needs certain types of packets. For a typical office installation, we're talking perhaps one day, two weeks max.

Want more information on AirSnort? Check out `http://airsnort.sourceforge.net`. Also take a look at `http://sourceforge.net/projects/wepcrack`.

AiroPeek

WildPackets Inc. offers AiroPeek 1.1, a utility that assists you in testing your Wi-Fi security. It can identify unauthorized clients and check encryption usage. It costs $1,995. Check to be sure that it works with your Wi-Fi hardware before investing in this utility. AiroPeek is a packet analyzer and it supports all higher-level network protocols such as NetBEUI, TCP/IP, and AppleTalk. Find more information at `http://www.wildpackets.com/products/airopeek`.

THE VPN SOLUTION

What does it cost to install a Virtual Private Network? Not necessarily any money, but surely some of your time. VPN technology is built in to all versions of Windows since Windows 95. (You have to add some free patches to Windows 95 and 98. We'll describe them in the section titled "Setting Up Your Virtual Private Network" later in this chapter.)

However, if your network is extra sensitive or extra busy, you might want to consider more robust VPN software from third-party vendors, or even purchasing dedicated VPN hardware.

Experts in Wi-Fi security say that Virtual Private Networks are the single best security measure that you can take. (We would argue that educating your personnel is at the top of the list.) A VPN provides encryption—a "tunnel" is drilled through the Internet and your messages are sent, scrambled, through that tunnel. VPNs do not provide 100% security." for Wi-Fi installations, but they, along with firewalls, are your best bet. (If you use VPN, you can just go ahead and turn off SSID, MAC, and WEP, as described earlier in this chapter.)

A VPN often does not require that you purchase additional hardware. The simplest VPN is merely a special kind of Windows dial-up connection you can define. It's just like the dial-up connections you already use to call your Internet service provider or indeed the connection to your Wi-Fi LAN. These dial-up connections are defined, and modified, in the Start, Settings, Network and Dial-up Connections dialog box in Windows 2000. (In Windows NT you'll find them in Start, Settings, Control Panel, then double-click the Network icon. For Windows 98 or Me, click My Computer, then Dial-Up Networking.)

We'll show you how to set up a Windows VPN connection in your computer shortly. If you're working on the other end (trying to set up a server that accepts incoming Wi-Fi connections to your corporate wired network) see Chapter 3, "Larger Scale Wi-Fi Setups."

A VPN offers several advantages to the Wi-Fi LAN user and manager:

- Administration of a VPN is centralized, minimized, efficient and highly scalable.
- You can use it to add security when connecting to your Wi-Fi LAN while you are nearby (close enough to connect over the air).
- You can connect via VPN from anywhere (remote access) by using the VPN to call into your corporate remote access server.
- VPNs are already installed on many enterprise networks.
- In addition to security, using VPN connections can save you money because you can make the connection to your LAN over the Internet (using a local phone call) rather than requiring your company to maintain adapters and other special hardware.

 All Wi-Fi client computers (a laptop using VPN to connect to your corporate remote access server, or even a desktop computer in an office) are exposed to intruders. You should use a firewall on each and every client computer. Like computers with always-on DSL and cable modem connections to the Internet, Wi-Fi client computers light up the night sky for hackers. Anyone who sees Wi-Fi client messages has the ability to attack the client computer. (See the sidebar later in this chapter "Installing a Firewall.") Also, a client computer should usually disable its sharing features (see Chapter 2).

Because it's designed to be the "business" operating system, and is the successor to NT, Windows 2000 offers the highest, most sophisticated security measures of all currently available Windows versions. Its encryption features for VPN connections are impressive. Choose Start, Settings, Network and Dial-up Connections, the name of your VPN connection. Then click the Properties button. Click the Security tab and you'll see the Port VPN dialog box (see Figure 8.1).

Figure 8.1
Here's where you can take advantage of Windows 2000's built-in security features for VPN connections.

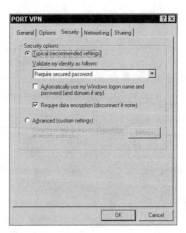

The options shown in Figure 8.1 include the two most useful computer security measures: authentication and encryption. Authentication means prove you are who you say you are. This usually involves a password/user name combination. Smart cards can also be used instead of that combination. Encryption means scramble the message so that if an intruder gets hold of it, it will make no sense to him. You'll want to be sure to check the Require Data Encryption check box shown in Figure 8.1. This is, after all, the primary reason to use a VPN for security.

The Windows 2000 Typical (recommended settings) VPN security option sets in motion an automatic series of communications between the client and server during a VPN connection.

Click the Advanced radio button, and then click the Settings button. You'll see the variety of options illustrated in Figure 8.2.

Figure 8.2
Use these options if you really know what you're doing.

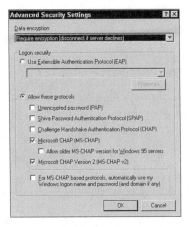

An explanation of the various options shown in Figure 8.2 is beyond the scope of this book. For all practical purposes—unless you are a Windows security guru—we suggest you choose the Typical security settings, which should be sufficient for most business installations.

SETTING UP YOUR VIRTUAL PRIVATE NETWORK

The popular ZoneAlarm firewall (described at the end of this chapter) will refuse to permit a VPN connection (see Figure 8.3). It should; that's its job. However, you can tell ZoneAlarm to allow VPN connections if you want. Other firewall software will behave similarly, getting its hackles up if a VPN connection request comes flying into your computer. One solution is to reduce ZoneAlarm's Internet security settings to the medium level. Or, if you have the Pro version of ZoneAlarm, you can open port 1723, and only that port.

Figure 8.3
The ZoneAlarm firewall is refusing to permit a VPN connection. It stands firm against unauthorized entry.

INSTALLING A WINDOWS 2000 VPN CONNECTION

1. Click Start, Settings, Control Panel, then double-click the Network and Dial-up Connections icon in Control Panel.

2. Double-click Make New Connection, then click Next.

3. Click the Connect to a Private Network Through the Internet radio button, then click Next.

4. If there is already a previously defined VPN connection in your computer, you can choose whether you want automatic dialing. The purpose of this option is to create an initial connection with an ISP, for example, prior to the VPN tunneling. If not, select the Do Not Dial the Initial Connection radio button, then click Next.

5. Type the host name or IP address of the computer or network to which you are connecting. The host name is the usual human-friendly address used to go somewhere on the Internet. For example, the host name of CNN is www.cnn.com. Alternatively, you can type the IP address, the synonym for the host name, expressed as a four-unit number, such as 24.28.244.19. Click Next.

Tip

Perhaps you want to give your IP address to someone else so he or she can tunnel to your server. To find out the IP address in a Windows 2000 computer, go to this Internet site:

http://northdelta.net/domainaddress.asp

If that doesn't work, go to www.google.com and search for "find my IP address."

You can use built-in Windows utilities to find the IP address of Windows 95, 98, and NT. We'll show you how to do this in the sections later in this chapter for those computers.

6. Choose one of these radio buttons. If you want this connection to be available to all users on your network, click For All Users. Click the other radio button if you want this connection limited to your use alone. You must be an Administrator to permit all users access to this connection. Click Next.

7. Type whatever name you want to give this connection (suggestion: Include the acronym *VPN*). Click Finish.

The connection dialog box will now automatically appear. To connect, click the Connect button. To see this dialog box in the future, click Start, Settings, Control Panel. Double-click the Network and Dial-up Connections icon in Control Panel, and then double-click the connection you want to use.

Tip

You can quickly create multiple VPN connections by opening the Network and Dial-up Connections dialog box (follow the previous step 1), then right-clicking one of the VPN connections and choosing Create Copy from the context menu. Right-click the new connection and choose Rename. Then right-click the new connection and again choose Properties so you can edit its properties. This way you can rapidly set up VPN connections for various security settings, various target servers, and so on.

INSTALLING A WINDOWS NT VPN CONNECTION

 NT requires that you install Service Pack 6a before setting up your VPN connection. SP 6a can be downloaded from www.microsoft.com/ntserver/nts/downloads/recommended/sp6.

1. Click Start, Settings, Control Panel.

2. Double-click the Network icon in Control Panel.

3. Click the Protocols tab. Click the Add button. You'll see the Select Network Protocol dialog box.

4. Select Point To Point Tunneling Protocol (this is VPN). Click OK.

5. Click Continue in the setup dialog box. At this point you might be asked to insert your Windows NT CD. After the necessary files are copied, the PPTP Configuration dialog will appear.

6. Click the drop-down arrow next to Number of Virtual Private Networks. Choose 1, then click OK.

7. Click the OK button in the Setup Message dialog box.

8. Click the Add button in the Remote Access Setup dialog box.

9. Select VPN1-RASPPTPM device, and click OK.

10. In the Remote Access Setup dialog box, select the VPN1 port and click the Configure button. Make Dial Out Only the only option selected for Configure Port Usage. Click OK.

11. In the Remote Access Setup dialog box, check to be sure that the VPN1 port is selected. Click the Network button.

12. Ensure that TCP/IP is the only option checked under Dial Out Protocols in the Network Configuration dialog box.

13. Reinstall the NT 6a Service Pack.

14. Shut down, then restart your computer.

Now you must create a dial-up networking phone book entry, by following these steps:

1. Click Start, Settings, Control Panel.

2. Double-click the Network icon in Control Panel.

3. Click New.

4. Under Name the new phonebook entry, type in whatever name you want to use for this VPN connection. (Suggestion: include the acronym *VPN*.)

5. In the Server dialog box, choose I am Calling the Internet, and then click Next.

6. In the Modem or Adapter dialog box choose RASPPTPM.

7. In the Phone Number dialog box enter the address of the server you want to contact. Click Next, and then click Finish.

Tip

Perhaps you want to give your IP address to someone else so he or she can tunnel to your server. To find out the IP address in a Windows NT computer, click Start, Run, type **cmd**, and click OK. This will display the command (DOS) window. Then type **ipconfig** at the command prompt (>). Press Enter. Your computer's IP address will be displayed.

8. In the Dial-Up Networking dialog box, select the new connection you just defined here in the Phonebook Entry To Dial. Drop down the list and click More. Select Edit Entry and Modem Properties.

9. Click the Server tab. Select the following options: TCP/IP, Enable software compression, and Enable PPP LCP extensions.

10. Click TCP/IP Settings. Select the following options: Server assigned IP address, Server assigned name server address, and Use IP header compression.

11. Click the Security tab. Select both Accept Only Microsoft Encrypted Authentication and Require Data Encryption.

12. Click OK to close the dialog box.

Using the VPN Connection in Windows NT

1. First connect to your Internet service provider as you ordinarily do when using e-mail or the Internet.
2. Open the Dial-Up Networking window (described in the previous steps) and select VPN server entry from the Phonebook drop-down list.
3. Click Dial.
4. Enter your user name and password.

Installing a Windows 98 VPN Connection

Microsoft has released an update for Windows 98 Virtual Private Networking (VPN) that addresses several known issues and is designed to enhance the protection of both dial-up and VPN connections by strengthening several aspects of password management and data encryption.

If you have Windows 98 SE (Second Edition) installed, you can skip this step (this update is included in SE).

This update, which was released in July, 1999, includes (and replaces) the Windows 98 Dial-up Networking Security Upgrade (Dun40.exe)

The Windows 98 Virtual Private Networking Update (Vpnupd.exe) is available from the following Microsoft Web site: www.microsoft.com/windows98/downloads/corporate.asp.

If want better security (and you should), an update is planned that will increase your Windows 98 VPN encryption from 40-bit up to 128-bit (for Windows 98 SE users only). To see if this update is available yet, go to www.microsoft.com/windows98/downloads and search for 128-bit.

Here's how to establish a VPN connection in Windows 98:

1. Start, Programs, Accessories, Communication, Dial-up Networking.
2. Double-click the Make New Connection icon.
3. Click Next.

   If this is the first time you've defined a connection, you'll be asked whether you want your modem detected. Agree if necessary, then follow the instructions to install the hardware on your machine.
4. Type into the Type a Name for the Computer You Are Dialing field whatever name you want this connection identified by. We suggest you use the acronym *VPN* somewhere in this name.
5. Click Next. In the Host Name or IP Address dialog box, enter the name or IP address of the server you want to call. The host name is the usual human-friendly address used to go somewhere on the Internet. For example, the host name of CNN is www.cnn.com. Alternatively, you can type the IP address, the synonym for the host name, expressed as a four-unit number, such as 24.28.244.19.

Tip

Perhaps you want to give your IP address to someone else so they can tunnel to your server using a VPN connection. To find out the IP address in a Windows 98 computer, click Start, Run, then type in `winipcfg`. Click OK. Your computer's IP address will be displayed, along with a label describing the name of this address. If you see more than one address listed, you're looking for the address label via which you want to receive incoming calls.

6. Click Finish.

7. Open the Dial-Up Networking window again (see Step 1), then right-click the name of your new VPN connection and choose Properties from the Context menu.

8. Click the Server Types tab.

9. Under Advanced Options, select the following options: Log on to Network, Enable Software Compression, Require Encrypted Password, and Require Data Encryption.

10. Select TCP/IP under Allowed Network Protocols.

11. Click TCP/IP Settings, and then select the following options: Server assigned IP address, Server assigned name server addresses, and Use IP header compression.

12. Click OK to close the dialog box.

To connect to your VPN in Window 98, follow these steps:

1. First connect to your Internet service provider as you ordinarily do when using e-mail or the Internet.

2. Now open the Dial-up Networking utility (see Step 1 in preceding step-through list).

3. Double-click the name of your VPN connection in the Dial-Up Networking window.

4. Enter your username and password.

5. Click the Connect button.

INSTALLING A WINDOWS 95 VPN CONNECTION

Microsoft has released an update for Windows 95 VPN, similar to the one described earlier for Windows 98. You'll need the Dial Up Networking 1.3 Performance & Security Update, available for downloading from
`www.microsoft.com/windows95/downloads/contents/WURecommended/S_WUNetworking/`
`dun13win95/Default.asp`.

And you'll also want the Windows 95 Virtual Private Networking Update (Vpnupd.exe), which can be downloaded from `www.microsoft.com/windows95/downloads`.

Here's how to create a connection to a VPN in Windows 95:

1. Locate My Computer, and then Dial-Up Networking.

2. Click Make a New Connection.

3. Type into the Type a Name for the Computer You Are Dialing field whatever name you want this connection identified by. We suggest you use the acronym *VPN* somewhere in this name.

4. Select Microsoft VPN Adapter in the Select a Device drop-down list.

5. In the Host Name or IP Address dialog box, enter the name or IP address of the server you want to call. The host name is the usual human-friendly address used to go somewhere on the Internet. For example, the host name of CNN is www.cnn.com. Alternatively, you can type the IP address, the synonym for the host name, expressed as a four-unit number, such as 24.28.244.19.

Tip

Perhaps you want to give your IP address to someone else so he or she can tunnel to your server using a VPN connection. To find out the IP address in a Windows 95 computer, click Start, Run, and then type in winipcfg. Click OK. Your computer's IP address will be displayed, along with a label describing the name of this address. If you see more than one address listed, you're looking for the address label via which you want to receive incoming calls.

6. Click the Finish button.

7. In the Dial-up Networking window, right-click the name of your new VPN connection.

8. Select Properties from the Context menu.

9. Click the Server Types tab.

10. Under Advanced options select the following: Log on to Network, Enable Software Compression, Require Encrypted Password, Require Data Encryption.

11. Under Allowed network protocols, select TCP/IP.

12. Click TCP/IP Settings, then select the following: Server Assigned IP Address, Server Assigned Name Server Addresses, Use IP Header Compression.

13. Click OK to close the dialog box.

To connect to your VPN in Windows 95, follow these steps:

1. First connect to your Internet service provider as you ordinarily do when using e-mail or the Internet.

2. Now open the Dial-up Networking utility.

3. Double-click the name of your VPN connection in the Dial-Up Networking window.

4. Enter your user name and password.

5. Click the Connect button.

USING FIREWALLS AND INTRUSION DETECTION

Several times in this chapter we've suggested that you should install a firewall. It is one of the most important security measures available to protect a network, or indeed, individual computers that are exposed to attach via Wi-Fi connections or always-on broadband Internet lines (DSL or cable modem).

Firewalls don't protect your data while it is being transmitted via Wi-Fi or over the Internet. Instead, a firewall is a way of protecting your computer so that an intruder cannot get into your hard drive or other data storage units. (Firewalls are also sometimes used by corporations to block or monitor their employees' access to the Internet or to hush-hush locations with a LAN or WAN—wide area network.)

Here's how a firewall works. It can be either hardware (a "firewall machine") or software, like the popular and powerful ZoneAlarm (see "Setting Up ZoneAlarm" at the end of this section).

When the information packets arrive at your network, most networks receive them using a packet filtering router (or screening router). This is a security feature that refuses to permit an outsider to connect to applications within the network unless the router knows that outsider (based on the outsider's Internet IP address).

More advanced routers can even use profiles to ID an incoming call. A profile includes the usual IP address, but also includes additional information about the call such as the protocol it's using (FTP versus HTTP, for instance), addresses being used, and other data. Beyond this, some companies even use two routers, on the theory that the more the merrier. This double-router system is called a *bastion host*.

> **Note**
>
> Do you sometimes get the feeling that computer security isn't yet perfected? Does the whole motley collection of computer security strategies and devices remind you of a big city apartment door with five chain locks, three deadbolts, and a fisheye peeper window? The more the merrier because no one tactic really does the job? If you feel this way, you're completely correct in your feelings. But back to security measure #422, firewalls.

Using a router can prevent even hackers who manage to get past lower-level protections. An additional level of security is provided by an "authenticating server" that works with the screening router. The authenticating server does pretty much what any other authenticating technology does: It verifies that the person using the outside IP address actually is known to you. Together, a screening router plus an authenticating server make up the most common firewall used in corporate security today.

Another approach is called a *proxy server*, which can check the contents of each data packet as it arrives at your network. However, this kind of checking can obviously slow up a system. Paradoxically, though, when used as a cache (holding area), a proxy server can improve the speed of Internet access. The proxy server can act the same way as a local, desktop computer's Web page cache: When you look at a Web page it is stored on your hard drive. Then, if you ask your browser to look at that page again (which happens surprisingly often), it can flash the stored page onto the screen rapidly. Hard drives are generally faster than accessing a page over the Internet. (To see your personal cache, choose Tools, Internet Options in Internet Explorer, then click the Settings button in the Temporary Internet Files section.) Be aware, though, that unless a proxy cache is periodically flushed of old data, it can cause a problem. Users can get old data that they are not aware *is* old.

We should also note a popular protocol (set of rules) you may want to look into. It's called *RADIUS* (*Remote Authentication Dial In User Service*). It can help you organize elements of your security. It assists you by maintaining lists of user names and associated passwords, along with other kinds of security data. When an outsider attempts to get in, RADIUS challenges them for the required authentication.

HARDWARE VERSUS SOFTWARE

Recall that firewalls can be hardware units, such as some Linksys Cable/DSL routers or Cisco's Secure PIX machine. Other firewalls are simply software such as Zone Labs' ZoneAlarm or Norton Security 2001.

Just how expensive the hardware firewall might be depends on your traffic. You can spend as much as six figures for one unit if your network handles heavy loads of communication. Hardware is also usually more scalable than software. If you are dealing with a very large, very intense network, you will likely want to use hardware solutions for various of your security needs. And if things start to slow down, add more servers or outboard firewall units. If you have lots of traffic, you've probably also got big money to throw at security machinery. Good for you. You might even want to consider subdividing your protection plan by giving security measures their own, separate hardware unit. This has an effect similar to parallel processing: It can greatly increase throughput.

Assign separate machines to focus individually on your various security jobs: Intrusion detection, the VPN, the firewall, and encryption can be separated into individual, dedicated hardware units. Although this is the most expensive tactic, it's also the most efficient, both in terms of strengthening security, as well as speeding up the process.

Software firewalls—given that they are one more utility manipulating network communications—are frequently responsible for slowing down traffic, particularly if there is only one server through which all messages must bottleneck.

INTRUSION DETECTION

Think of firewalls as deadbolts: They're there to keep people out. But if someone does get in—perhaps through the notorious back door—you might also want to have an intrusion detection system (IDS) active as well. Think of an IDS as a motion detector that sits in your house and sets off a honking alarm if anyone is moving around. They got past the firewall, so now it's time to take direct steps to deal with them.

IDS security also comes in both hardware and software versions. If you're interested in an IDS system, they are available from Cisco, Check Point, Symantec, Computer Associates, and others.

SETTING UP ZONEALARM

If you are installing a SOHO Wi-Fi LAN, or otherwise feel that you don't need the fortress-level authentication and firewall security described earlier in this chapter, perhaps you'll want to consider using ZoneAlarm on your Wi-Fi computers.

Free to individual personal computer users, $19.95 to $40 per seat for business, government, or education customers—ZoneAlarm is a popular solution (14 million users) for those concerned about possible intrusion into their computers. It works on Windows 95, 98, NT 4.0, or Windows 2000.

Of all the personal firewall software we've seen, this is currently the best one. It's tight, solid, highly effective in cloaking your machine, thoughtfully designed, easy to install and use, informative, and sturdy as a 12-foot steel wall. Turn it on and relax. That's our advice. ZoneAlarm has a perfect price, too: $0.00 for individual users.

ZoneAlarm is a software-based firewall that can stand firmly between your quivering, vulnerable little hard drive and the big, bad, outside world that wants nothing more than to breach your security and run amok. As you know (if you've been reading this book sequentially), hackers, crackers, and whackers and their creepy robot assistants are constantly roaming the Internet, looking for broadband, always-on Internet connections. And then there's the odd fellow out there holding a laptop who keeps waiting for a bus that never comes.

ZoneAlarm features three security levels you can specify against incoming messages, and it also lets you define which of your applications have permission to access the Internet. Beyond browsers and mail readers, some other applications, such as RealPlayer or Word, can connect to the Internet. Some applications regularly connect to the Internet—without even asking you—and send data. Do you like that? (Remember that a firewall can both guard against attempts to get into your system from the Internet, but also against attempts to get out onto the Internet as well.) If an application does try to access the Internet, ZoneAlarm lets you know. At this point you can permit, refuse, or establish a rule for the future so you don't have to respond each time that software makes the attempt.

One of ZoneAlarm's best features is that you can tell it to completely disable all Internet activity. If an attack is underway, pressing Ctrl+S immediately slams steel sheets down over all your virtual doors and windows. ZoneAlarm instantly locks all Internet communication. Or, you can set the lock to take effect automatically after an interval of inactivity (just the way a screensaver, or power saver, activates if you haven't used the keyboard or mouse for a while). This way, a broadband always-on Internet connection is no longer always on.

But even while you're actively surfing the Internet, connected to your Wi-Fi LAN, e-mailing or otherwise communicating and vulnerable, ZoneAlarm protects you very effectively. Port-probing spiders, scanner bots, and little men on bus stop benches will find nothing but invisibility and silence if they try to get into your computer. Evil pings, knock-knock-knocking on your virtual doors over the Internet will see and hear nothing at all. It's as if your computer isn't powered on, or doesn't even exist at all.

Follow these steps to install ZoneAlarm:

1. Type this address into your browser: www.zonelabs.com/support.htm
2. Choose whether you want the free or Pro version, and then click the appropriate Download Now or Free Download button to start the download.
3. When asked, choose to save the file to your hard drive (note where it's being saved).
4. Locate the Zonealarm.exe file on your hard drive and double-click it to install.
5. Click Next several times to complete the steps for installation.

If you want, ZoneAlarm starts automatically each time you power up your computer (we recommend this). Like most good software, this option, and many others, can be changed to suit your personal preferences. (Note that many computer professionals, and many ordinary people, leave their computers turned on all the time to prevent thermal shock from the initial power up surge. This prevents chips and other hardware from premature failure.)

One of the authors of this book has been using ZoneAlarm with his cable modem connection for a year and has found an average of six electronic knocks on his computer's door per hour. Worse, this pinging activity goes way up, very fast, if you visit certain types of sites. For instance, sites like Napster that deliberately open some of your directories to permit sharing files can dramatically increase incoming access requests.

When you do get pinged, somebody (or their robotic crawler agent) is trying to access your computer. ZoneAlarm can keep a log of these attempts so you can read it and weep. It can also sometimes provide you with details about the source of these attempted break-ins.

SECURITY SUMMARY

How much security you need depends on the sensitivity of your data, and your pocketbook, but everyone needs to pay attention to security issues.

There are two primary categories of computer security, and all computer owners should address them at some level:

- Corruption of your data (viruses)
- Exposing your data (loss of privacy)

None of us wants worms, creepers, spiders, viruses, or other lower life forms running around in our hard drives or networks. So you do want to warn your personnel to take the obvious steps against infection (don't open e-mail attachments without checking first with the sender; don't download and run programs from unknown sources). Install a firewall. Frequently back up your documents and other data. Antivirus software is more a psychological comfort than a true defense, in our opinion.

The second security issue is privacy: You don't want strangers reading your files. The best protection against peeping is encryption. However, the security measures built into Windows and ordinary Wi-Fi equipment are insufficient. If you're at all serious about protecting your Wi-Fi LAN, you'll certainly want more than spread spectrum, Wired Equivalent Privacy, MAC, and the like.

In addition to their inherent weaknesses as encryption, you also have to manage keys (with WEP and similar encryption systems). Managing keys can become impossibly burdensome if your Wi-Fi LAN grows in size beyond a rather small group of people. The best solution to these problems is to increase the quality of the encryption by using a 128-bit (or better) scheme. Also you can automate the connection process so you don't have to face the keys problem. Both of these problems are solved if you install the right Virtual Private Network. Our bottom line advice: Install a VPN and firewalls. How robust your VPN and firewalls can be depends on your needs, fears, and, above all, on your pocketbook.

Finally, and most important, be sure to teach your personnel the fundamentals of security. No matter how much time, money or hardware you throw at the security problem, it can all be rendered useless if you have a single foolish employee. You are in big trouble if someone on your Wi-Fi LAN has loose lips, or is willing to loan their Wi-Fi enabled laptop to a stranger in Starbucks for a few minutes. A few minutes is all it takes to right-click the VPN dial-up connection in Windows, see the properties of your heavily guarded Wi-Fi VPN, and later knock down all your carefully constructed protection systems.

THE WI-FI REVOLUTION

In this chapter

Most experts agree that someday wireless communication will dominate information services. We will enjoy HDTV, broadband Internet, videophone, and all the other modern communication systems—free at last from the need to use any wires.

Until that happy day arrives, many forward-looking people are connecting their computers with Wi-Fi, an early taste of what the future holds. People want to be free to roam around their offices (or indeed around the country) and still remain connected to their network, their e-mail, and the Internet.

AN UNSTOPPABLE TREND

There is an inexorable shift taking place from wire to wireless. More and more people are retiring their old mice and keyboards for optical wireless versions. Expectations have been raised: The nearly universal acceptance of, first, cordless phones, then later cell phones, has conditioned us to expect freedom of movement during all our communications. The idea that we have to be physically connected to information sources may soon become as outdated as the picture of mom, pop, sis, and junior gathering around the 50 lb. wooden Philco family radio to listen to the Masked Avenger broadcast.

Of all the wireless technologies—Bluetooth, Home RF, HiperLAN/2, and others—the 802.11 technology (Wi-Fi) seems destined to be the clear winner. In America, it has already gained what most observers consider unstoppable momentum, having more or less rolled over Home RF and Bluetooth already. HiperLan/2 also seems doomed (See "What About HiperLAN/2" later in this chapter.)

Interestingly, Wi-Fi is now even being built into some notebooks. Some models include onboard Wi-Fi electronics, so you don't need to purchase a Wi-Fi PCM card, nor have it poking out from the side of your portable. Toshiba's new 4600 Pro model even features a built-in Wi-Fi antenna, embedded in the frame around the screen.

LOWERING COSTS, INCREASING SALES

The cost of Wi-Fi gear has decreased rapidly. Two years ago, Wi-Fi PC cards typically cost around $600 and access points were in the $1,700 range. And for these prices, you got equipment that was 10 times slower (1Mbps) than units that now sell for around $100 (cards) and $200 (access points). Of course, Wi-Fi hardware has not yet come down to the same price range as wired Fast Ethernet NICs, which currently go for around $45. Nonetheless, by early 2002, Wi-Fi LAN units are predicted to cost 50 percent less than today, so the cost of setting up a Wi-Fi LAN should by then be comparable to ordinary ethernet.

Along with the ongoing price breaks, sales of Wi-Fi equipment have ramped up fast: Optimistic experts predict that what was a $1.2 billion wireless LAN market in 2000 could grow to more than $5 billion by 2005. Wi-Fi is one of the few strong, vital areas amid the debris of the general tech collapse.

Wi-Fi LAN technology is currently installed and working in approximately 30% of American companies, according to a recent survey. And an additional 25% of IS managers expect to install Wi-Fi soon. Why is business moving to Wi-Fi LANs? Primarily because you actually save money. It costs a lot of money to extend a wire LAN, after the walls have been plastered, painted, and hung with all those pictures of Our Founder. Also, productivity gains result when WLANs free employees to move around the building without having to leave their computers behind.

Today, Wi-Fi networking is a practical, affordable, often clearly superior alternative to traditional wire networking. And the Wi-Fi revolution is only in its early stages. The next step in Wi-Fi—expected within months--is the availability of ultra-high-speed Wi-Fi equipment: boasting throughput five to ten times faster than today's already speedy Wi-Fi standard.

When a technology enjoys rapidly improving features and rapidly declining prices, that technology is on the familiar trajectory, which launched such now-pervasive conveniences as television or indeed personal computers.

If Wi-Fi seems destined to be an important element in the future of communications, the coming 802.11a specification is the future of Wi-Fi.

Is Wire Doomed?

Will Wi-Fi perhaps completely replace wire networking the way cell phones seem destined to eventually replace fixed phones? No, says John Richey, Senior Technologist at Agere Systems. "Access points still need wires, and server-side communications benefit from the speed and reliability of wired networks." However, he points out that for users moving from office to office, it makes sense to use Wi-Fi. And for home, office, and public space uses like e-mail and Internet Wi-Fi in notebooks is fast becoming the de facto standard. Richey points out that many OEMs (Original Equipment Manufacturers) are embedding Wi-Fi in their products. The technology is found across Dell's whole line, and it is built to order in IBM, Gateway, HP, Compaq, and other computers.

A Peek Into the Near Future

The 802.11a Wi-Fi standard is expected to replace the current 802.11b standard relatively quickly. The new technology isn't inherently any more costly (though early adapters who have to have the latest, greatest hardware will, as always, get stuck with extra R&D costs). Also, the 11b antenna will not work with 11a; you need a second, specialized 5GHz antenna.

Nonetheless, 802.11a units running at between 54–100 Mbs in the 5GHz band offer compelling advantages. The 54Mbs speed is the Wi-Fi specification standard; some manufacturers claim speeds up to 100Mbs when their equipment goes into "turbo" mode.

Not only do 802.11a units offer throughput that's five to ten times faster than today's Wi-Fi, they also use the 5GHz band. That frequency band is free of interference from HomeRF, microwave ovens, cordless phones and other gear that can impede communications in the current 2.4GHz band. (The 2.4GHz band is one of three radio spectrum bands known as the ISM bands, for *Industrial, Scientific, and Medical*, which should give you a clue that they are potentially a bit crowded.)

By the way, it's possible that there might be an intermediate step between today's 802.11b and 802.11a. Also on the horizon is another version of 802.11, *802.11g*, which works in today's 2.4GHz band, but claims throughput of over 20Mbps. 802.11g is a standard proposed by Intersil, the leading 802.11 chip maker, and others. (A version of 802.11g was recently approved by the IEEE.)

Nobody knows whether 802.11g will be a brief stop on the way to 802.11a, or of it will take us longer to reach 11a than is currently predicted, or if 802.11a will even become popular at all. Perhaps the strongest argument in favor of 802.11g as a transition technology is that it is backward compatible with 802.11b. 802.11g does not offer new technology; it's simply about twice as fast as today's 802.11b.

802.11a, however, relies on a different, incompatible modulation scheme. While there are certainly advantages to moving 802.11 out of the 2.4GHz spectrum (such as freedom from interference by household appliances and other devices), there are potential problems with the 5GHz spectrum proposed for 802.11a, including possible difficulties getting regulatory approval for the spectrum usage.

Yet another technology on the horizon is 3G, which is as yet vaguely conceptualized, and primarily intended for cell phone transmissions. If it becomes a reality, and broadband transmissions are possible to and from cell phones, there is no reason to think that the cell phones of the future that use 3G won't become more like today's computers. However, unlike the 802.11 technologies, 3G does not have wireless networking in mind as its primary emphasis.

Whatever standard prevails in the future, 802.11b is here now, and works well!

Caution

Just as TVs are sold with an "ideal" viewing area spec, so, too, are Wi-Fi throughput specs usually rather generous when compared to actual real-world data transfer speeds. When you buy a 19" monitor, the "actual viewing area" as they call it is around 17". Two inches doesn't sound like much, but in fact a 17" screen is 20% smaller than a 19" screen. Similarly, the 11 Mbps data transfer rate usually cited for today's Wi-Fi units actually averages around 4Mbps true throughput in the ordinary office environment.

WHO CARES ABOUT THROUGHPUT?

Who cares about greater throughput? When you can send a whole book of data in seconds with today's Wi-Fi, what's the point of boosting speeds by an order of magnitude? People who ask questions like this are in good company. Bill Gates once asked why anyone would ever need more than 640K of system RAM memory.

One answer to the "why more speed?" question is such media as HDTV. Typical computer digital streaming TV may need only 5Mbps, but full HDTV transmission needs 20Mbps. Add such niceties as real-time, big screen video conferencing, high-bandwidth multicasting, and as-yet-uninvented high-bandwidth multimedia uses and your data pipeline can never be too fast or too wide. Your wireless equipment has to be able to accommodate the high-bandwidth data that will be dumped into your home and office via satellite and fiber optic cable.

Another, more comprehensive answer to the need for speed is simply that the more throughput you achieve, the more users you can service simultaneously, at lower costs, requiring less power.

Tip

By the time you are reading this book, Wi-Fi manufacturers are expected to have released 22Mbps firmware (software that you download from the Internet and that is then sent over your Wi-Fi LAN to your Wi-Fi access point units). This firmware upgrade is all that is necessary to roughly double the current 11Mbps data transfer rate.

CH
9

WHO CARES ABOUT ENERGY?

With the typical Wi-Fi unit broadcasting at around only 100 milliwatts, you might be excused for thinking that worry about powering Wi-Fi is a non-issue. True enough, powering Wi-Fi doesn't matter when you're connected to an electrical outlet, but one of Wi-Fi's *raisons d'etre* is portability.

There's the rub: Powering anything, including Wi-Fi gear, from the battery in a portable computer isn't a free lunch. One of the main advantages that Wi-Fi offers is the freedom to roam away from a desk yet remain connected to a network. Portables, of course, can be forced to depend on battery power while you are roaming. Most Wi-Fi cards come with power-conserving features, including software that helps put them into sleep mode when active communication isn't required. Some Wi-Fi cards cache messages following brief bursts of communication. New low-power chip designs are capable of reducing Wi-Fi power consumption by over 80 percent.

THE WEIGHTLESS COMPUTER

You've seen those old-time pictures of gramps and the family around that Philco radio. In most technologies the early physical devices are *heavy*. That wooden Philco was bulky and cumbersome. It took nearly half a century for radios to transition from 57 pound family console models to earpiece portables weighing only ounces. Radios had to wait for the invention of transistors and ultra-light batteries.

We're now some twenty years into the evolution of personal computer technology and we're only just now getting featherweight titanium portables. Most portables still demand heavy battery packs and cannot yet communicate wirelessly. But the day is coming when computing will be as light and free as those featherweight FM radios people hang on their ear.

Bill Gates called it "information at your fingertips." Others have predicted the eventual replacement of personal computers with a "virtual desktop." After all, what's *personal* on your computer isn't the hardware, or even the software. Practically everybody has RAM chips, Internet Explorer, and Word. What's personal about your computer is your *information*—your list of Favorite Web sites, the documents you wrote, the e-mail you received, and so on.

Just as Wi-Fi—or a technology like it—promises to free you from your hardware, so, too, does the Internet promise to free you from your software. Many expect that much if not all your applications—as well as your documents and other personalized data—will migrate from their current locations on your hard drive and find their way onto the Internet.

DISTRIBUTED COMPUTING

There are already early signs that this migration is happening. Programmers are increasingly writing *distributed* applications. What that means in a nutshell is that instead of writing a single program that is installed on single hard drives, a program is broken up into pieces that communicate and cooperate over the Internet. For example, the billing part of an invoicing program might reside on a server in an accounting department in Toledo, but the part of this application that actually mails invoices might be located on a computer at a fulfillment house in Santa Barbara. What's more, the invoices might be first generated by software on a server farm in Tampa that accepts orders from customers via a Web site. These three pieces of software are actually one virtual program—parts of what traditionally would have been a single application residing on a single personal computer.

Now, though, with high-speed Internet communications, there is no reason not to split an application between machines located in the upper Midwest and both coasts. They can function as smoothly together as if they were all together on a single machine. Software divided like this into communicating parts located on different computers is known as an *n-tier application*.

FREEING UP YOUR DATA

After you understand that the trend is away from unified information processing and storage, there is no longer any reason for *your* data to be localized either. This frees you in several ways. For one thing, the less information you must carry with you, the less battery power you need and the lighter your information machine becomes. *Lighter* in the sense that the unit weighs less, but also lighter in the sense that you need no longer "find a plug" for the power source, or, with Wi-Fi, find a telephone jack. In the future, you'll likely be able to walk into Starbucks, but also walk anywhere in the mall, or even anywhere outside—and your lightweight computer will never lose its connection to your information or your applications.

Remember, it's your personal data that really matters; not the hardware and not the software. You should be able to look up a phone number anywhere, and using *any* machine: your GameBoy, your sister's HDTV, the screen built into your desk at work. The hardware should simply not matter. After all, you don't think of the TV sets in your house as "personal" TVs, they are simply devices you use to get information that interests you. It doesn't matter— and it shouldn't matter—whether you are watching your own TV or one in a sports bar. Likewise, it shouldn't matter where or how you are connected to the Internet.

SUBSCRIPTION INFORMATION SERVICES

Another trend in distributed information is the current interest in putting applications on the Internet, and charging you a subscription fee to use them. Instead of taking up space on your personal hard drive, Word will sit on someone's server somewhere (you never find out who or where, and you don't care, any more than you care about the location and ownership of Channel 10).

Anytime, anywhere, you can run Word and it will always be the latest, most bug-free version. The implications of Internet-resident applications for Wi-Fi users are clear: with information processing tools like Word moved off hard drives and into "the air" your Wi-Fi device becomes lighter still and your ability to roam increases that much more.

When you stop to think about what the Internet really is, it becomes clear that it represents a significant new paradigm. Sun boss Scott McNealy has famously predicted that "the network is the computer." Part of what he means is that information is increasingly being separated from a single, physical location and left to float within a dynamic, expanding worldwide virtual machine.

With Wi-Fi, broadband always-on Internet connections, and the seemingly unstoppable growth of online data, the traditional distinction between being online and offline is increasingly blurred. Computing is turning outward from classic hard-drive-oriented data processing to the Internet, that rich and measureless database.

BLURRING DISTINCTIONS

An underlying principle of much of today's software is that, in theory, you should experience no real distinction between your hard drive and the Internet. You should be able to easily manage or retrieve information either locally or worldwide, without having to use different tools or techniques. Features like Windows Explorer's Find utility should operate seamlessly in both realms. And, indeed, they do. For example, take a good look at the toolbars in the Windows 2000 Explorer. You'll find that you have the Internet Explorer address bar and Internet links bar right there (if you don't see them, right-click a visible toolbar and select them). Click an Internet link and Windows Explorer morphs into Internet Explorer.

It should be no surprise—just based on their names—that Internet Explorer and Windows Explorer are morphing into a single, all-purpose entity. They're not quite *totally* integrated yet, but they're almost one. While in Internet Explorer, choose View, Explorer Bar, Folders. There's your hard drive contents.

The goal is clear: You are interested in information, purely. You do not care if you are connected to "your" Internet Service Provider, or the ISP hired by the Venetian hotel in Las Vegas—you just want to verify your reservation and get down to the real business at hand: the slots.

People should be able to navigate, search, store, manage, and retrieve information— independent of specialized hardware, and regardless of where you are currently located.

With the ongoing blurring of the distinction between the hard drive file manager and your Internet browser, you now need to learn how to use only a single tool. Notice that if you modify your favorites or links in Internet Explorer, those changes are visible in Windows.

Eventually, given the constant implosion of applications into a single, all-purpose information processing tool, we can expect that eventually your Wi-Fi device will be light enough to let you just "turn the dial" and select an application. And as soon as you "tune" to your application, a list will be displayed of all your documents, customizations, favorites, and other data relating to that application. And none of this will reside in a memory device on your Wi-Fi unit.

There are obvious advantages to freeing up your information, not least of which is that a Wi-Fi device can then become an omni-purpose tool. After all, you don't have one car that you use to drive to the dentist, and a separate car you use to pick up groceries.

WIRELESS FREEDOM OF INFORMATION

Wi-Fi is at the forefront of today's information revolution. Just as the Internet can free you from having to carry information storage devices around with you, so can Wi-Fi free you from having to plug into phone lines or wired network nodes.

To detach yourself from hard-wired and hard-drive–based computing, you have to adjust to some new ways of thinking. It's easy enough to plug a Wi-Fi PCM card into your portable and then get used to answering your e-mail out on the sun deck. Moving from your office to, let's say, poolside, is not a burden. Most of us make that kind of adaptation quite easily. After all, what's a veranda for?

Other changes, though, can require some mental rewiring. Until this year, when I traveled, I had to be sure that each hotel had a data-ready phone (and that their switchboard didn't foul up my connection to the Internet). Then I had to write down the local phone access numbers for my ISP so I didn't have to run up long-distance charges to get my e-mail. As soon as I got a cable modem, though, it became clear that my ISP was not able to offer local e-mail access numbers (being a cable TV company they simply don't use the *phone* as their connection device). In fact, they didn't offer a long distance number I could call either. The solution? I got an Internet-based e-mail account with MSN's Hotmail. That way, I bypass my ISP entirely. All I have to do is connect to the Internet to get e-mail via my browser (no phone call, no e-mail program—just the trusty Internet).

As you have seen in this book, Wi-Fi connection points are spreading to coffee houses, hotels, airports and, it seems likely, soon to a location near you. It shouldn't be long before most places are "lit up" and you can just flip the power switch on your Wi-Fi unit. You'll still have to worry about being stuck in the Bates Motel, Limping Hawk, West Virginia, of course, but you always have to worry about places like that anyway.

In addition to moving my e-mail onto the Internet, I've also been thinking about freeing up some hard drive space by uploading those giant photo and music files as well. Check out www.myplay.com's "music locker" feature or if you're interested in megabytes of free online storage space, try one of these sites: www.freedrive.com, www.zden.com, www.myspace.com, `www.filesanywhere.com`, or `www.xdrive.com`. Internet storage can also be a good way to back up your data, if you find a storage site that you trust.

What About HiperLan/2?

Several technologies are challenging Wi-Fi today, though most experts expect Wi-Fi to prevail in the end, at least in the United States. The most serious current competitor for the wireless computing market is HiperLAN/2. However, there are no books written about it and you probably have never heard of it. (That's HiperLAN/2's problem in a nutshell: It has not been widely publicized or promoted in the United States.)

CH
9

Expected to be available in the first half of 2002 (*after* the rollout of high-speed 802.11a products), the HiperLAN/2 technology is coming here from Europe. Developed by the European Telecommunications Standards Institute, HiperLAN/2 is quite similar to 802.11a. They both operate at 54Mbps in the 5GHz band. HiperLAN/2, however, is targeted at data, video, and voice transmission. Although 802.11 technology so-far has focused on data, that could change. Voice and video are certainly possible.

Unlike 802.11a, however, which only offers support for IP over Ethernet, HiperLAN/2 offers several modes including Point-to-Point Protocol, IEEE 1394, IP over Ethernet, and asynchronous transfer mode.

Some marketing analysts predict that HiperLAN/2 could catch on in Europe. The devices are being built via a joint venture between Nokia and Ericsson. John Richey, however, observes that "HiperLAN/2 is losing a lot of ground right now...there are going to be no vendors supporting it." The problem with HiperLAN/2, he says, is that "you want a product that works globally." People want to be able to take their portable back and forth across the seas without having to worry about the wireless standard. Also, Richey points out, HiperLAN/2 technology "doesn't scale well for multimedia...it's targeted for voice applications."

There is reason to suspect, however, that—given their similarities—HiperLAN/2 and 802.11a technologies could simply *merge*, thereby preventing a costly, wasteful, and eventually pointless transcontinental economic war for the wireless computing dollar (or Euro, as the case may be).

To be perfectly blunt, HiperLAN/2 and 802.11a have much more in common than do 802.11b and 802.11a. It might clarify things to point out that HiperLAN/2 and 802.11a both use the same orthogonal frequency division multiplexing. Mention *that* at your next social outing and see who your real friends are.

VoIP: The New Telephone?

HiperLAN/2 offers voice communications in addition to data, but there's no reason that voice cannot be transmitted over 802.11a or even 802.11b systems.

If you've ever tried to use a regular Internet modem connection to make a long distance call, you've probably been disappointed. I have a friend in Athens and we got so frustrated with the feedback and delays that we went ahead and spent the (considerable) money to make a traditional telephone call.

Nonetheless, VoIP (Voice over IP-based data networks) may come into its own with wide-band IP systems. In addition to ordinary voice calls, VoIP can also handle FAX and even permit you to annotate data documents with audio voice notes. Multimedia, too, can become an integral feature of an efficient VoIP technology.

Even though VoIP is getting some attention these days from both consumers and industry, there remain some problems to be solved before this technology reaches its potential. Transmission quality must be significantly improved. Latency and even packet loss are also challenges facing those who are trying to bring VoIP successfully to market. As with many of the topics raised in this chapter, only time will tell how—or whether—VoIP succeeds.

11,000Mbps Impulse Radio

Some are predicting that late 2001 the FCC will throw open the floodgates and permit Ultra-WideBand (UWB) transmissions for short-range wireless transmissions. This technology is radically different from the competitors for the wireless market now dominated by Wi-Fi. Nonetheless, UWB has to be considered a potential threat to Wi-Fi, even though UWB has actually been around for forty years. Here's the story.

UWB made its debut back in 1962 with the discovery that high-speed *impulses* could be used to communicate information, instead of traditional radio *wave* transmission techniques. The government quickly slapped security restrictions on impulse communication systems research, and did not lift this classified status until 1994.

Manufacturers have been busy beavers since 1994 and the curtain is about to go up. UWB equipment is now ready for FCC approval after 40 years of experimentation, and intense R & D during the past seven years. The UWB technology has now been built into devices that display little blinking green lights, indicating *science at work* to us average people.

Not to get too technical, but here's a brief moment of UWB physics: These units generate *subnanosecond pulses*. Luckily, electronics—antennas, oscilloscopes, and such—were developed in the late 1960s that could sense these minute excitations (the impulses) and measure them. In other words, information could be transmitted via radiated excitations. Sending out quanta of information, versus classic wave-based transmission.

UWB pulses are extremely brief, and they need very little power as well (only a few milliwatts, which is about 1/10,000th the power used by cell phones that put out .6 watts, or Wi-Fi gear which transmits at about 250 milliwatts). Another plus is that UWB employs fundamentally simpler electronics than the traditional radio technologies.

Data can ride on UWB pulses because the pulses are time modulated: digital 1 is indicated by a pulse that arrives at the antenna just a little earlier than it should; digital 0 arrives a little bit late.

I suggest you don't bother your pretty head trying to understand any more about the physics, or even the electronics, underlying UWB. I'm certainly not going to go any further than necessary into UWB theory.

What you *do* need to know is that UWB—if it does come to market—offers transmission speeds that dwarf even the new 802.11a throughput, even in its "turbo" mode. UWB can reach 11,000Mbps, compared to today's Wi-Fi 11Mbps speeds.

As always, the ideal specifications have to be tempered by real-world applications. In the case of UWB, the first units approved for marketing by the FCC are expected to be limited to speeds closer to 100Mbps, operating at ranges of around 100–200 feet. There is nothing in the technology, however, that limits UWB to these speeds and these distances. That's why some see UWB as the future of LAN and PAN (personal area networks) communications.

There are a couple of other rather interesting features the UWB offers, besides ultra high speed and ultra low energy costs. As you know, our homes and bodies are being continually shot through with billions of waves—some natural like neutrinos, some artificial like radio, radar, TV, satellite, and cell phone signals.

Experts claim that because it involves low excitations (or something), UWB radiations will not interfere with other signals. Nor will it even require allocation of a band for its use. This is *ultra-wide bandwidth* technology. It operates *across the entire frequency spectrum* rather than requiring its own, particular band. Bandwidth limitations of radio technologies restrict how many signals can be broadcast simultaneously. Not so with UWB.

Over the years the airwaves have been subdivided by the government into thousands of "bands:" a band here for trucker talk on CB radio, a band there for satellite TV, another band up there for FM radio, and so on. It's as if you had a highway with 50,000 lanes and the FCC decided where to lay down all the dividers to prevent bedlam.

Things are different, though, with UWB. The government isn't being asked to allocate a new lane of traffic. It's being asked to *permit* UWB transmission *everywhere*. UWB can use *all the other existing bands* (a wide spectrum like that associated with noise from devices like a monitor). However, UWB broadcasts are not invasive (in theory anyway)… other communications are untouched by UWB for the same reason that the radio signals from Rock 92 FM do not interfere with automobile traffic. Cars and FM radio waves are simply so unlike in size and speed that they may as well be in different universes, even though technically they "share the road" physically.

UWB sends very high-speed excitations, bursts of data so rapid that they zap right through the other, slower communications without disturbing them at all. In theory, anyway. The FCC has been accepting the results of experiments for some time now, and seems favorably disposed. Nonetheless, there is concern that some UWB devices have the potential to interfere with some important communications bands, including air traffic control, TV, and others. Proponents of UWB claim that any such interference is easily eliminated by tuning the UWB broadcast. Time will tell.

If you're interested in pursuing UWB further, check out the Ultra-Wideband Working Group at www.uwb.org.

CH
9

Welcome to the Wireless World

The Wi-Fi revolution is real, and it is liberating. After you've tried it, you won't want to go back to your old ways. Your computing devices no longer need to be tethered to wire networks, and your data need no longer live on a hard drive in a heavy desktop machine. In other words, wireless networking as implemented in 802.11 makes true distributed computing possible. This is great stuff! Your freedom to work where you like is greatly enhanced.

There are many mundane advantages to Wi-Fi technology. These tend to fall along the lines of not needing to knock down walls for wiring networks and greater freedom about where computers and information resources are located. But perhaps the greatest benefit of this technology is that it is enabling to the human spirit and extends our ability, capacity, and dreams—in the same way that the build-out of the Internet infrastructure is powerful and enabling. With neither technology do we yet fully understand all that is possible, and many of the best innovations are yet to come.

One of the best aspects of Wi-Fi wireless technology is that it is inexpensive and easy to use. In this book, we've given you a road map to implementing Wi-Fi networking in your home and office (as well as in public Wi-Fi locations like Starbucks coffee shops). We hope you enjoy your adventures with Wi-Fi. Welcome to the wireless world!

IDEAS AND RESOURCES

TECHNICAL NEWS

http://news.cnet.com/news/0-1002.html

www.zdnet.com/

www.pcworld.com

WI-FI TECHNOLOGY

www.wi-fi.com (Wireless Ethernet Compatibility Alliance [WECA])

www.telecoms-mag.com/issues/200009/tcs/understanding_wireless.html

www.ieee.org/

www.bawug.org/ (Bay Area Wireless User Group)

www.zdnet.com/enterprise/filters/resources/0,10227,6016597,00.html (ZDNet Wireless Resource Center)

searchnetworking.techtarget.com

www.wirelessdevnet.com/

www.nsrc.org/wireless.html

www.cc.gatech.edu/fce/hardware/wireless/wireless-details.html

winweb.rutgers.edu/pub/

www.ubig.com/parctab/

www.ubig.com/hypertext/weiser/UbiHome.html

SECURITY ISSUES

www.cs.umd.edu/~waa/wireless.html

www.isaac.cs.berkeley.edu/isaac/wep-draft.pdf

WI-FI VENDORS

www.convergedigest.com/WiFi/WirelessLANVendors.htm

www.wirelessethernet.org/sponsors.asp

www.wirelessethernet.org/certified_products.asp

www.orinocowireless.com/

www.aironet.com/

GLOSSARY

802.10—An IEEE standard establishing specs for security in both wired and wireless LANs.

802.11—An IEEE standard establishing specs for Wi-Fi communications.

802.11a—The next step in Wi-Fi technology. This specification allocates three 100MHz sub-bands in the 5GHz region for unlicensed Wi-Fi use. Transmissions operate at speeds up to 54Mhz.

802.11b—The current Wi-Fi technology. This specification allocates three 100MHz sub-bands in the 5GHz region for unlicensed Wi-Fi use. Transmissions operate at speeds up to 11 Mhz.

Access Point (AP)—Hardware that connects a Wi-Fi LAN to an existing wired network. You can have multiple access points in a large office, overcoming the transmission distance limitations of Wi-Fi and permitting users to roam with their laptops throughout a big building (and outside) while remaining connected to the Wi-Fi LAN.

Ad Hoc Network—Also known as a peer-to-peer workgroup, this is a Wi-Fi LAN that has no central access point unit; instead, only PCM cards (or USB devices) stuck into the various computers communicate with each other.

Application Layer—Networks, like database software and other computer phenomena can be subdivided into "layers" (or zones). The application layer is the combination of hardware (a workstation or local computer in this case) and software (a program such as a browser) which, together, offer a network user the ability to communicate with that network by sending e-mail, attached files, browsing Windows Explorer, and so on.

Application Software—*See Application Layer.*

ARQ (automatic repeat request)—An error correction technique. Incorrect data is detected and the receiver requests a retransmission of the problem frames.

Authentication—Verifying identity. One form of authentication is typing in a user name and password. The Wi-Fi spec offers two kinds of authentication: open system and shared key. *See Open System.*

Band—A range of frequencies in the RF (radio frequency) spectrum. (Sometimes called a frequency band.) Two or more simultaneous transmissions on the same frequency or band of frequencies can interfere with each other. Therefore, an international regulator (International Telecommunication Union (ITU)) and an American agency (FCC) have divided the whole RF spectrum into bands. Further, these regulators also specify the transmission broadcast pattern, and the maximum permitted transmission power (which determines the distance the transmission will travel). These rules are intended to ensure that radio traffic moves smoothly with a minimum of interference.

Here are the current primary bands, their range, and typical uses:

- **Very low frequencies (vlf)**—3 to 30kHz. Time signals from Denver and elsewhere, "Atomic clocks," and "radio controlled clocks" from Radio Shack.

- **Low frequencies (lf)**—30 to 300kHz. Navigational systems, radio broadcasting, and marine (water) communications.

- **Medium frequencies (mf)**—300 to 3000kHz. Same as lf. AM radio in the United States employs the band 535 to 1,700kHz.

- **High frequencies (hf)**—3 to 30MHz. Shortwave radio, CB radio, and HAM radio.

- **Very high frequencies (vhf)**—30 to 300MHz. TV, FM radio (which is a band within the TV band). When you tune to 91.5 Raleigh Public Radio, you are listening to a frequency of 91.5 megahertz (millions of cycles per second). The radio station's transmission unit is vibrating like there's no tomorrow: 91,500,000 cycles per second. You can "tune" your receiver to this precise frequency. (Frequency means "how often" and you can see that these little critters vibrate pretty often to broadcast FM.) FM radio's allocated band in America is 88 to 108MHz. TV channels 2–6 are located between 54–88MHz and TV channels 7–13 are located between 174–220MHz.

- **Ultra high frequencies (UHF)**—300 to 3000 MHz (3 GHz). Wi-Fi, UHF TV, HAM, outer space communications.

- **Super high frequencies (SHF)**—3 to 30 gigahertz (GHz). Next generation Wi-Fi. Satellite and outer space communications.

- **Extremely high frequencies (ehf)**—Range from 30 to 300 GHz. Amateur radio, satellite, and earth and space exploration are among the users of this band.

There are hundreds of allocated bands. Here are a few examples of equipment that has its own radio frequency band: alarm systems; garage door openers; radio controlled airplanes and toys; the space station; GPS units; baby monitors; wildlife radio tags; deep outer space communications, and many others.

Bandwidth—The width of a band of electromagnetic frequencies. All transmitted signals—natural, analog, or digital—have a bandwidth. You can think of bandwidth as the amount of data that is transmitted per minute (second, millisecond, or any unit of time measurement you want to use).

Basic Service Set (BSS)—A group of Wi-Fi units working together as a LAN (ten or fewer units, most likely). When you assign a network name (SSID) to your Wi-Fi equipment, you are thereby identifying the BSS to which it will belong. Each Wi-Fi unit in a given BSS must use the same SSID. *See ESS.*

Baud Rate—How fast a digital signal travels (measured as the number of pulses per second).

Bit Rate—The number of bits transmitted in one second.

Bluetooth—A wireless standard that never really caught on with the consumer. In contrast to Wi-Fi, which easily extends hundreds of feet (and further with specialized equipment), Bluetooth is intended for appliance-to-appliance communication of not more than thirty feet. (Think of it as the infrared beaming mechanism intended for data exchange between PDAs on steroids.) Bluetooth is also far slower than Wi-Fi. A typical Bluetooth communication involves a Bluetooth-enabled PDA that automatically synchs with your desktop PC. For more information, see www.bluetooth.com.

Bridge—The part of a network that connects one local area network (LAN) to another LAN, with both using the same communication protocol. *See Router.*

Broadband—Also called *wideband*, this is a relatively generous (wide) band of frequencies. Just as a really wide door permits more people through per minute than a narrow door, broadband permits more information to be transmitted per minute (or whatever unit of time you want to use to measure throughput). Cable modem Internet connections, for example, are broadband. With a broadband, a signal can be *multiplexed*: divided into several frequencies then transmitted simultaneously on more than one path.

BSS—*See Basic Service Set (BSS).*

Carrier Current LAN—A LAN that uses the electric wires in a building to transmit data.

Center for Devices and Radiological Health—A scientific organization that tests for damage to humans resulting from radiation emitted by electronic products (such as cell phones and Wi-Fi units). A division of the U.S. Food and Drug Administration.

Coaxial Cable—Coax is a cable with a central metal wire surrounded by shielding that prevents interference. Used by cable TV as well as in older ethernet networks.

Cyclic Redundancy Check (CRC)—A way of sending a checksum-like number (technically the data's value is divided by a polynomial and the remainder is then sent along with the data). The receiver does the same division and sees whether the transmitted remainder is the same as the one that the transmitter sent. If they are not identical it is likely (though not certain) that there was an error in transmission and a request to retransmit can be sent.

Data Encryption Standard (DES)—The most widely used encryption system to hide information for business and less-than-top secret government and military communications.

DES is almost impossible to crack (it's not yet been cracked, though in theory it can be). DES uses sixteen cycles of encipherment, and some cryptanalysts have gotten as far as cracking everything up to the fifteenth cycle.

The strangest feature of DES is that its algorithm (way of doing its job) was made public. That was one of the government's requirements: Everybody would get to see how the whole thing worked!

IBM developed an algorithm code-named *Lucifer* (*cifer*, get it?) that is not that hard to understand if you're a programmer: It employs a series of elementary transformations (using logical operators such as XOR) on the bits in the plaintext and the key. Lucifer employed many such transformations, but individually they are quite familiar and understandable. It's the combination of so many of these simple transformations that makes DES the strong system it is, just as many simple twists of hemp strands can become a rope strong enough to hold a battleship to a dock.

Everything from inter-bank money transfers to cloak-and-dagger correspondence is now being enciphered using DES. By 1987 DES had become the standard for financial and other institutions worldwide and it still has no serious competition.

DES does a real Cuisinart job on the characters in a message. It uses both substitution and transposition, as do most all encryption systems of any sophistication. In other words, it substitutes one character for another, and it also moves the characters around so they're not in their original order. These two fundamental enciphering techniques are sometimes called *confusion* and *diffusion*.

Text is divided into individual 8-character blocks. DES then enciphers each block differently, depending on how the *previous* block was enciphered. This creates a cascading effect—a kind of amplification of the enciphering process. If you change a single character anywhere within the original text, all the following blocks are changed as a result. That, combined with the fact that DES works on bits rather than bytes (characters), considerably expands the "alphabet" being used. DES churns out ciphertext that to an outsider appears close to totally random. The original message has been *smeared* until it is no longer information. It has become mere noise.

Decibel (dB)—The ratio of one value to another. The ratio often involves sound—such as the ratio of silence to noise when measuring the racket at an airport. Like the Richter scale, which measures earthquake strength, the dB scale is exponential. It goes up fast: 10dB is 10 times the power, but 20dB is 100 times stronger. DB can also be used to specify signal gain, or loss. For instance, the average indoor Wi-Fi transmitter loses about 20dB every 100 feet between itself and the receiver. This loss escalates exponentially as you increase the distance between the transmitter and receiver (now you see why the decibel scale is exponential itself). The dB scale employs the legendary formula: log(ratio)*10.

Direct Sequence Spread Spectrum (DSSS)—DSSS modulates the RF signal and spreads the transmission over the entire frequency band allocated for Wi-Fi communication.

DSSS adds a redundant bit pattern to accompany each bit that is transmitted. This redundant pattern is called a *chip*. The precise code used to generate these chips is kept secret, in theory, from anyone other than the authorized sender and receiver hardware (users are not involved in this automatic encryption process). However, outsiders can rather easily crack this primitive security scheme. The actual value of adding this redundant code is that the chip contains enough information about the original bits that those bits can be reconstructed should they be dropped, mangled, or lost in the noise, during transmission. Put another way: Adding DSSS is a way of coping with environments suffering from noise and interference, so having to retransmit dropped bits can be avoided. Unfortunately, though, sharing the 2.4GHz band with Wi-Fi units are wireless telephones that *also* employ spread spectrum technology. Spread spectrum transmissions are "louder," so to speak, and therefore easier to receive through noise. *See FHSS.*

DSSS—*See direct sequence spread spectrum (DSSS).*

ESS—*See Extended Service Set (ESS).*

Electronics Industry Association (EIA)—An American group made up of many U.S. electronics firms that endeavors to set standards for equipment.

Ethernet—A popular LAN technology that operates at speeds similar to Wi-Fi (10Mbps). IEEE 802.3 is the standard that defines ethernet behavior.

Extended Service Set (ESS)—A group of Basic Service Sets linked together by a common distribution system.

FHSS—*See Frequency Hopping Spread Spectrum (FHSS).*

File Transfer Protocol (FTP)—A TCP/IP protocol used to transfer files.

Firewall—Software, or less often hardware devices, specially configured to handle incoming calls to a network from the outside. Firewalls (a.k.a. Venus flytraps) receive special attention from system administrators. If it is a separate machine, it is the guard at the gate and it does not contain any sensitive files, although it can host bait files. Often the firewall has multiple incoming lines, and only one, highly supervised, line going from the firewall into the company's network. Of course the concept of a *firewall* has grown over time to include more than simply a dedicated, gateway machine. Firewalls are now commonly utility software that guards the connection between a network and the outside world. Software-based firewalls are most commonly used in SOHO installations (small home or office LANs or individual Internet connections).

A firewall not only governs attempts to get into your system from the Internet or outsiders communicating via Wi-Fi or other transmission systems, but it also can block or log attempts to get out onto the Internet from as well.

When the information packets arrive at your network, many networks receive them using a "packet filtering router" (or screening router). This is a security feature that refuses to permit an outsider to connect to applications within the network unless that outsider is known to the router (based on the outsider's IP address). More advanced routers can even use *profiles* to ID an incoming call. A profile includes the usual IP address, but also includes additional information about the call such as the protocol it's using (FTP versus HTTP, for instance), addresses being used, and other data. Beyond this, some companies even use two routers, on the theory that the more the merrier. This double-router system is called a *bastion host*.

Using a router can prevent even hackers who manage to get past lower-level protections from using applications on the network. An additional level of security is provided by an "authenticating server" that works with the screening router. The authenticating server does pretty much what any other authenticating technology does: It verifies that the person using the outside IP address actually *is* the person allowed to use that address. Together, a screening router plus an authenticating server make up the most common firewall structure used in security today by major corporations.

Firmware—Something between hardware and software, it's physical (it's a computer chip called a PROM for programmable read-only memory). However, it is also software in the sense that unlike ROM (read-only) memory chips, PROM can be reprogrammed. Many Wi-Fi cards and access point units include PROM chips. That way, if the manufacturer makes an improvement to the software in the card or unit, you can download that software from their Web site, run it in your main computer, and it will automatically seek out your Wi-Fi and transmit itself to the Wi-Fi card or unit, thereby upgrading your hardware without having to send it back to a service center.

Frequency Hopping Spread Spectrum (FHSS)—Both FHSS and DSSS (see previously in this appendix) employ frequency-shift keying and spread-spectrum radio waves. Spread spectrum technology modulates and spreads data across the entire allocated frequency band. FHSS differs from DSSS in that both transmitter and receiver are synchronized so they hop from channel to channel using the same, agreed-upon pseudorandom sequence. There are 78 possible hop sequences and 79 usable channels. If one channel is noisy, the transmitter and receiver leap over to a clear channel. DSSS chips are not used in the FHSS scheme.

FTP—*See File Transfer Protocol (FTP).*

IEEE—*See Institute of Electrical and Electronic Engineers (IEEE).*

Independent Basic Service Set Network (IBSS Network)—A Wi-Fi LAN also known as an ad hoc network because there is no need for an access point or any backbone infrastructure.

Industrial, Scientific, and Medicine Bands (ISM Bands)—The 2.4GHz band is one of three bands known as the ISM frequency bands, for *Industrial, Scientific, and Medical*, which should give you a clue that it's potentially a bit crowded. The FCC allocated 902MHz, 2.400GHz, and 5.7GHz for these purposes.

Institute of Electrical and Electronic Engineers (IEEE)—A nonprofit organization that establishes standards and offers other services for a large number of technologies ranging from dams and electric power to biomedical, telecommunications, and consumer electronics fields. The IEEE boasts members from over 150 countries. IEEE describes itself as a group that "helps advance global prosperity by promoting the engineering process of creating, developing, integrating, sharing, and applying knowledge about electrical and information technologies and sciences for the benefit of humanity and the profession."

IP—Configuring or finding out your IP address. *See WINIPCFG.*

IPCONFIG—*See WINIPCFG.*

LAN—Local Area Network. A relatively small, self-contained network. As opposed to WAN (Wide) or PAN (Personal).

Modulation—Distorting a wave to make that wave convey information. Sine waves are used in radio communications, but a sine wave is quite regular: It goes up and down much like the wave pattern that spreads when you drop a stone into a pond. To make these consistent, uniform patterns carry information, you must deform them somehow. It is similar to the way that striking a drum conveys a rhythm by interrupting its regular vibrations from time to time. There are several kinds of modulation, and each is more interesting than the previous. Here are the three most common modulation techniques:

- Pulse modulation (PM) turns the sine wave on and off, sending bursts...pieces of sine waves. Radio Shack's "radio controlled" clocks get their time signals via PM. PM can travel great distances. The time signals sent out from the Denver transmitter easily cover the entire United States.

- Amplitude modulation (the AM in AM radio) modifies the voltage, changing the "height" of the waves. The pattern produced by a singer's voice can be applied to the sine wave and thereby transmit the words and tones of that voice. The video (not audio) portion of over-the-air TV transmissions is sent via AM as well.

- Frequency modulation (FM radio, TV sound, cell phones, and many other electronics devices) varies the number of times (the frequency) that the sine wave oscillates per unit of time. Think of moving your hand up and down in the bathtub to create waves, then speeding up and slowing down your hand pulses. FM has the advantage of not being distorted by the static caused by ever-present lightning strikes (that travel far) and other sources of static interference, such as an angora sweater worn by someone flailing and flipping around.

Network Basic Input/Output System (NetBIOS)—The primary standard communication software used by LANs.

Network Interface Card (NIC)—A card plugged into the inside of a computer (in a slot) to physically connect the computer to a network. The NIC usually also does some data processing of its own. Wi-Fi cards are usually PCM cards designed to be plugged into portables, but there are adapter cards that plug into a computer's PCI slots, then you plug the PCM card into that adapter.

NIC—*See Network Interface Card (NIC).*

Node—A connection point in a network. It can be an endpoint like a NIC, or a place where traffic is redistributed, such as a router.

ODBC—*See Open Database Connectivity (ODBC).*

Open Database Connectivity (ODBC)—A standardized database interface (an API, application programmer's interface) that attempts to solve the age-old problem of databases with different internal structures, different ways of labeling and storing their contents. The programmer writes an SQL query and ODBC rewrites the query to make it understandable to a particular database. Each different database (Access's Jet, dBASE, ordinary delimited text, whatever) has its own ODBC driver, just as each different computer monitor has a driver dedicated to assisting it in communicating with Windows. A programmer writing an application that needs to interact with a database can write standard ODBC commands (essentially SQL queries). These queries are then translated by ODBC into language understandable by the particular database being queried at the time. It's all rather sad. The lack of database standards causes many inefficiencies like this, slowing up program execution and bedeviling programmers. There should be a single, standardized database structure for the same reasons that there is a single, standardized set of traffic signs used throughout the United States. Unfortunately, each company that works with databases wants to invent its own twists and offers a proprietary database schema. XML is the latest effort to sort things out and provide common standards. I'm not hopeful. People are already busy as beavers "improving" the XML standards. SQL is a language devoted to retrieving information from databases ("Give me a list of the phone numbers of all our salesmen in Boston who earn over $12,000 per sale." And other queries like that.)

Open System Authentication—The IEEE 802.11 specification supports two kinds of authentication (guaranteeing someone's identity so you know they are one of "your own" who legitimately can log on to the Wi-Fi LAN). The *Open System* authentication first requires that a message be sent from the unit trying to get onto the LAN. This message is supposed to identify the requesting unit. Then the receiving unit (an access point, for example) replies saying "I know you" or "I don't recognize you." The receiving unit has the option of permitting access to only those identities on a list it has, or permitting *all requests*. The latter open-door policy is used in airports, coffeehouses, and other places that sell Wi-Fi Internet access to all comers.

The alternative Wi-Fi authentication system is called Shared Key (see elsewhere in this glossary). Both systems have, alas, proven lame and easily defeated.

PCM card —*See Personal Computer Memory Card International Association (PCMCIA or PCM).*

PCMCIA —*See Personal Computer Memory Card International Association (PCMCIA or PCM).*

Peer-to-Peer Network—A LAN where there is no central server, just a group of connected "clients." In a home, for example, you might have a computer in the study, in the Palace of Chaos, Junior's bedroom, and a portable. None of these is a server to the others, but you can LAN them together and permit them to share their files, Internet connections, and peripherals such as printers. They can share as equals, as *peers*. This type of LAN isn't too scalable, however. Larger networks require more formal structure and interactions based on more complex rules than found in a peer-to-peer setup.

Personal Computer Memory Card International Association (PCMCIA or PCM)— Standards describing three physical interfaces, ordinarily used with portable computers. There are Type I (3.3 millimeters), Type II (5.0 millimeters), and Type III (10.5 millimeters). Wi-Fi cards are usually PCM cards.

Pulse Code Modulation (PCM)—A technique that converts analog signals (often voice) into a digital bitstream.

Roaming—The ability to remain connected to a communication source, while moving. In Wi-Fi terminology, it means that you can keep a connection to the Wi-Fi LAN while walking around through a building, for instance, and going beyond the range of a single access point. As you stroll through a big Wi-Fi LAN building with multiple access points, your portable periodically check to see whether it is still in touch with its original access point or whether it should seek out a new one. When the signal from the original access point weakens enough, a new connection point is (hopefully) noticed, registered with, and connected to. All this is supposed to happen automatically without the human having to do anything.

Repeater—Acts like an amplifier, increasing the distance that data can travel over a network.

Router—A utility (sometimes software, sometimes hardware) that sits at the point where two or more networks connect within a WAN (Wide Area Network). The router's main job is to decide where to direct a packet of data, to move it further toward its ultimate destination in the WAN. Routers are placed at gateways (the point where one network touches another). As you can imagine, the biggest WAN of them all, the Internet, contains many busy little routers humming all the day and night long. Routers also keep information traveling along relatively efficient routes by acting like scandalmongers and tittle-tattle gossips. Routers keep a list of any bad routes that a traveling packet of data had to endure. If it finds any bad routes, it immediately updates its list of routes, makes copies of the list, and it *sends those lists to all its neighbor routers*, just like the town gossip. This technique is called the Routing Information Protocol (RIP).

Routing Information Protocol—*See Router.*

Server—A computer in a network that usually has greater hard drive capacity, greater speed, more RAM memory and greater security than the *clients* it serves. The server provides storage and information processing services for software that resides in the client computers. The clients (sometimes dumb terminals or workstations) interact with the user.

Service Set Identifier (SSID)—*See Basic Service Set (BSS).*

Shared Key Authentication—Only Wi-Fi units that have a secret, encrypted key can be admitted into the Wi-Fi LAN when they try to join it. The access point or receiver unit authenticates by comparing the requesting unit's transmitted key to a list of known-good keys. This system has weaknesses, and has proven lame in real-world situations.

Signal-to-Noise Ratio (SNR)—A communication performance measurement derived by dividing signal power by noise power. The result is expressed in decibels and the higher the ratio, the clearer the connection (because there is more signal, less noise). SNR is a spec provided for high-fidelity music equipment, as well as wireless networking and telecommunications transmissions.

Simple Mail Transfer Protocol (SMTP)—The protocol used to transmit e-mail on the Internet.

SMTP—*See Simple Mail Transfer Protocol(SMTP).*

SOHO—A relatively new acronym, meaning small office/home office. Often refers to telecommuters and their warrens, dens, or lairs located only feet from their bedrooms where they, like many authors, go for a nap whenever the mood strikes them. Wi-Fi LANs are ideal for this type of person and any family they may have.

SNR—*See Signal-to-Noise Ratio (SNR).*

Spread Spectrum—*See DSSS.*

SQL (Structured Query Language)—*See Open Database Connectivity (ODBC).*

SSID—*See Basic Service Set (BSS).*

Structured Query Language (SQL)—*See Open database Connectivity (ODBC).*

Throughput—How much data you can transmit over a network (or phone lines). Throughput is specified in characters-per-second, or other "units of data sent/per unit of time passed" measurements, such as bit rate or baud.

Transceiver—A device that both transmits and receives.

WECA—Wireless Ethernet Compatibility Alliance, an industry organization promoting and certifying Wi-Fi products. Members include Zoom, 3Com, Dell, Aironet, Agere, Nokia, and Nortel.

WEP—*See Wired Equivalent Privacy (WEP).*

Wideband—*See Broadband.*

WINIPCFG—The utility used by Windows 95/98 and Me to configure or find out your IP address (this is your unique Internet address while you are connected, or your unique Wi-Fi LAN address while connected to *that* network). For those lucky enough to have cable modems or other high-speed Internet connections, your IP address remains *static*, the same week after week, month after month. In any case, you may need to give your IP address to someone who might want to connect to you via NetMeeting or some other Internet communication utility. Or you might want to see your Wi-Fi IP address. If you're running both, you will have two separate IP addresses, one for Wi-Fi and another for your Internet connection. To see your IP address(es), run a DOS (Command Line) session in your Windows 95/98 or Me computer, then type WINIPCFG at the command line prompt (>) and press the Enter key. Windows NT and 2000 users should type IPCONFIG instead.

Wired Equivalent Privacy (WEP)—An optional IEEE 802.11 security technology that is a failure; it has been cracked. The "Wired Equivalent" part refers to the claim that this Wi-Fi security is as good as wired networks enjoy. One thing that the comparison seems to ignore: There is no physical barrier in Wi-Fi (a hacker can sit outside your office building and receive your Wi-Fi transmissions). Beyond that, WEP is inherently flawed for several reasons, not least of which is that Wi-Fi passwords are usually static (for convenience, people keep on using the same password instead of changing it periodically). For an in-depth report on the collapse of WEP security, see "Weaknesses in the Key Scheduling Algorithm of RC4" by Scott Fluhrer, Itsik Mantin, and Adi Shamir. Also see Chapter 8, "Security and Encryption," in this book for details about AirSnort and other WEP attackers. AirSnort, for example, requires that between roughly 100M–1GB of Wi-Fi data be captured (by the dude outside your building). Once sufficient data have been gathered, AirSnort requires less than a second to figure out the encryption password you are using.

Wireless Metropolitan Area Network—Wi-Fi links between buildings, creating an ad hoc WAN.

Wireless Medium—The air.

WLAN—A Wireless LAN (Wi-Fi LAN). A network composed of computers networked using radio communication rather than traditional wires. For more information, read this book.

INDEX

NOTE: Before using the CD-ROM read \readme.txt.

Installation Instructions

Windows 95/ NT 4

Insert the CD-ROM into your CD-ROM drive (see Note at bottom).

From the Windows desktop, double-click on the "My Computer" icon.

Double-click the icon representing your CD-ROM drive.

Double-click the icon titled START.EXE to run the multimedia user interface.

NOTE: If Windows 95/NT 4.0 is installed on your computer, and you have the AutoPlay feature enabled, the Start.exe program starts automatically whenever you insert the disc into your CD-ROM drive.